A GUIDE TO

Better Photography

NIGHT VIEW   BERENICE ABBOTT

A GUIDE TO

Better Photography

BERENICE ABBOTT

CROWN PUBLISHERS 1941 NEW YORK

PRINTED IN THE UNITED STATES OF AMERICA
BY J. J. LITTLE & IVES COMPANY, NEW YORK

Table of Contents

Acknowledgment

I acknowledge gratefully the help of all those who have made this book possible, including photographers who have generously provided examples of their work for illustration and publishers who have allowed me to quote from books on the history, technic and philosophy of photography. I wish to thank the Metropolitan Museum of Art *and the* Museum of Modern Art *for permission to reproduce photographs from their collections, and the latter for permission to quote from its publications. Thanks are also due various organizations, especially* RCA, Westinghouse, Eastman, Deardorff, Life, *and* Fortune. *Individuals who have been most helpful are* Beaumont Newhall, *curator of the department of photography of the* Museum of Modern Art; Ansel Adams, *its vice-chairman; and* Willard D. Morgan, *editor of numerous photographic publications. To* Elizabeth McCausland, *my warm thanks for invaluable assistance in the preparation of the manuscript.*

BERENICE ABBOTT

Illustrations

A GUIDE TO

Better Photography

1. What is Photography?

PHOTOGRAPHY is a new way of seeing, a new way of making pictures, made possible by the fact that light produces a chemical reaction on silver salts. Light reflected from real objects in nature is registered with many variations by applying this principle. Film (with silver salts in emulsion) is placed in the camera (a lighttight box) and light is admitted through the shutter (a light-controlling device.) The record of the original image may then be reproduced many times. But photography is more than this simple chemical and mechanical procedure to photography. During its century of life, it has been called "photogenic drawing," "the pencil of nature," "sun painting," "sun pictures," "shadow catching," all variants of its literal meaning (from the Greek) of "drawing with light." But photography is not only drawing with light, though light is the indispensable agent of its being. It is modeling or sculpturing with light, to reproduce the plastic form of natural objects. It is painting with light, to create the subtle tones of colors in nature. The synthesis of these effects evolves photography's uniquely photogenic character.

Photography's new way of making pictures has been put to a thousand uses, so that today its new kind of pictures serve a multitude of purposes. Photography celebrates themes infinitely more varied than those celebrated by old ways of picture-making. From X-ray photographs made at 1/30,000 of a second and step-by-step photographs of a brain operation to the soaring heights of aerial photographs mapping China's Great Wall, photography has widened the visual world to an extent unimagined by the exploring intelligence of fifteenth century picture-makers, i.e., painters and graphic artists. The widening has been not only by invention—knowledge of X-rays, stroboscope, higher powered lenses—but also by the application of human thought and feeling to photography. Seeing the unseen is not only a matter of machine and high speed flash; it is a matter of the imagination, of seeing what the human eye has been too lazy or too blind to see before.

The new picture, the photograph, has evolved a new creative vision. In the fifteenth century, vanishing perspective was developed to express the Renaissance feeling of vast seas to be charted, its diminishing distance a visual equivalent of psychological wonder. In the twentieth century, perspective is no longer a convention of geographical exploration; it is a reality of optics. It is a reality, moreover, susceptible to varied interpretations, as the photographer chooses. If distortion suits his purpose, he may distort. If he wishes the lens' vision to equate the eye's, he may correct distortion. The option permits him to accept psychological familiarity or to reject it, if thereby he intensifies his picture's emotional impact.

Photography's subtle yet seemingly simple character partly explains its universal appeal. Roots strike deeper, however, to wellsprings of individual endeavor and interest. Why do Americans spend more than a hundred million dollars a year on photography? Because photography is a useful science, an expressive art, a pictorial language with countless applications. This explains the professionals. But they are only a handful of the 15,000,000 estimated to use cameras in the United States. Hobby, recreation, adjunct to another profession, these reasons account for photography's tremendous popularity. The answer is: photography is fun.

The hunger for beauty, for self-expression, is age-old. Dance ceremonials of communal peoples are a form of mankind's search for beauty. The painting on velvet taught in female seminaries a century ago (now highly prized by collectors) expressed a similar desire. In our time, men and women gratify their artistic sense by turning to photography, newest of the arts and perhaps most responsive to the age's spirit. What is beauty? How does the average man see it? Through the ages, humanity has made images, memorials, souvenirs, to commemorate loved ones. During the past hundred years, photography has produced millions of portraits, ranging from masterpieces by Hill and Nadar to snapshots taken at Coney Island or Pike's Peak on a No. 120 roll film. Indeed, according to Taft's estimate in *Photography and the American Scene,* between 15,000,000 and 20,000,000 daguerreotypes were made in the United States during the period of the daguerreotype's greatest popularity. The souvenir, the sentimental record, is not an inferior order of the creative impulse; it feeds on the deepest springs of human emotion and memory. The album of Civil War days, with its fading tintypes of boys who never came back, was such an expression. Steichen's classic portrait of the elder Morgan represents the other end of the scale. Both kinds of portrait, from the souvenir to the masterpiece, recite valuable truths about the past.

Visual remembrance of past happy times is an equally real desire. Cruises, motor trips, weekend outings, of holiday mood, are no small part of recollected recreation and pleasure. To make and keep a record of them is the motive of hundreds of thousands of photographers. But beyond these motives, there is that deeper need for self-expression. In every human being, there are capacities for creative action. Often circumstances of life do not allow them to develop fully. Reality of work may be monotonous and dull, because it does not allow imagination and initiative to flower. Even the fortunate mortal who has found a perfect marriage between job and creative ability may find that his work goes better if he has change and relief. This need of human beings is almost as deep-seated as their need for air to breathe and food to eat.

The fact that you are reading this book shows that for you photography is a creative outlet. The fact, indeed, that you are doing photography at all proves it. But for whatever reason you are interested in photography and however you became interested, there is always a day of reckoning. Since the census does not take statistics of photographers, as it does of the photographic industry, it is impossible to say accurately how many of the 15,000,000 simply jumped into the vast sea of photography and learned to swim to save their lives. It is safe, however, to guess probably nine-tenths. With what results? If you are satisfied to click the shutter and accept what the corner drugstore photofinishing department hands back, then we don't need to go into the question. But if blurred, tilted, light-struck, underexposed negatives and prints do not give you the creative "lift" you seek, then you have come up against the reality of photography. At this moment in your life as one of the 15,000,000, you either throw away your camera and take to Chinese checkers, or you have a little heart-to-heart talk with yourself.

Whatever you want to do in photography—rise to professional status, add it to your profession as in medicine, architecture, writing and painting or simply fulfill the hunger for beauty—you are now at a crucial point.

A spiritual inventory is in order; for you will photograph better, more creatively, more happily, if you take the trouble to learn how. Contrary to the idea of many, photography is not an involuntary reflex, like the heart's beating or the lungs' breathing. It is the product of centuries of scientific investigation, culminating in the creation of a machine and a method with unique capacities for making pictures. But only when the machine and the method are guided by a human being can the photograph be made. In the widest sense, human intelligence creates photography. To make a photograph expressive of what you feel and think is a cumulative experience. Learning how involves all the creative faculties. After that, wider use of skill becomes increasingly rewarding.

But, *How can I learn how?*, you may ask. The answer is: by mastering the photographic process step by step. When you have sufficient technical knowledge to broaden your application, then the adventure of photography really begins.

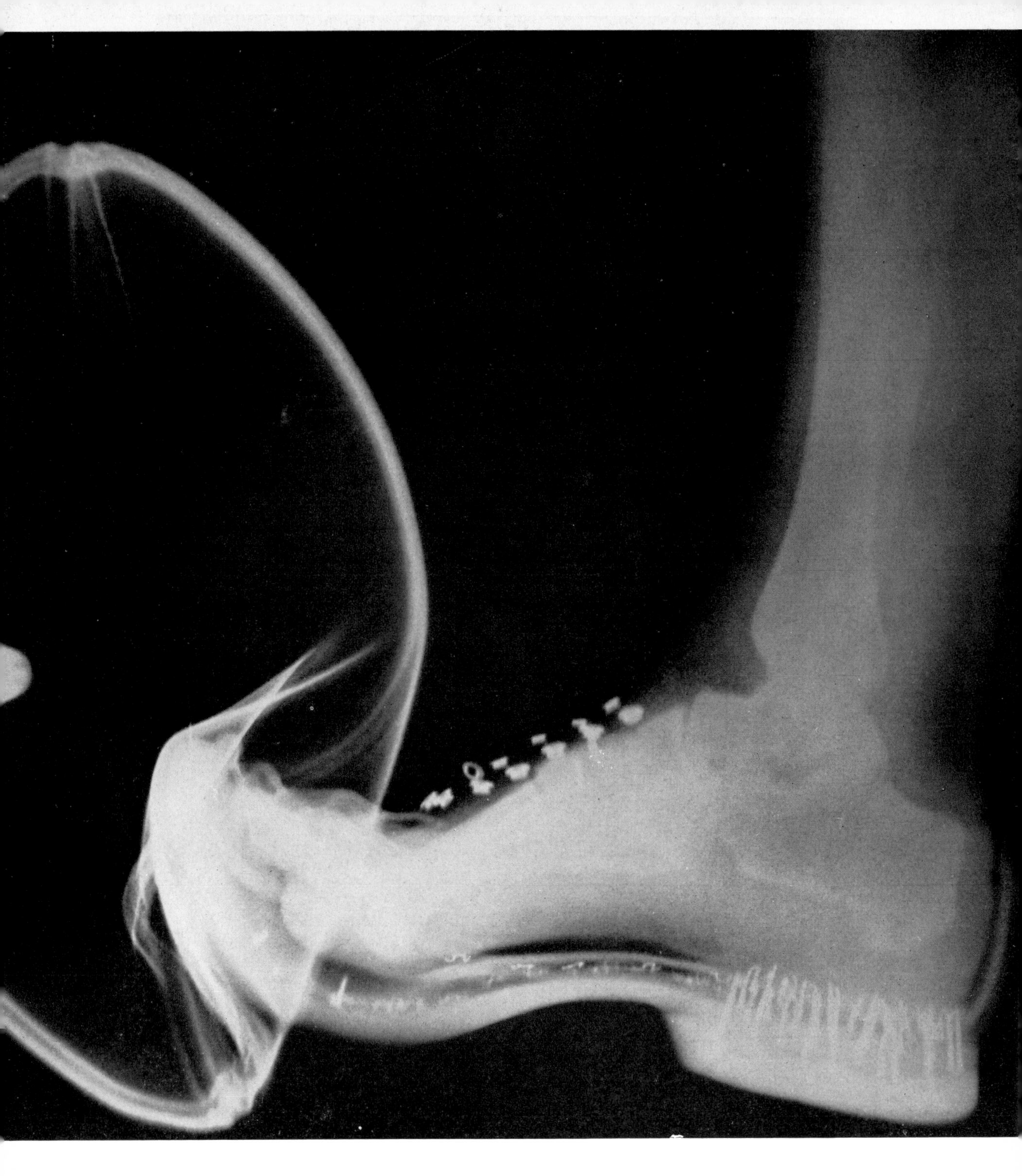

2. FOOTBALL BEING KICKED — Westinghouse ultra-high speed radiograph taken by DR. CHARLES M. SLACK

Eastman ultra-speed X-ray film in a casette with Patterson Hi-Speed intensifying screen; exposure, 1 microsecond (1/1,000,000 second); 65 kilovolts (65,000 volts); Eastman X-ray developer.

Courtesy of Westinghouse Electric & Manufacturing Co.

3. LOLA MONTEZ — Southworth & Hawes

Daguerreotype. Lola Montez (1818-1861) was an Irish-born dancer, actress and adventuress, and, toward the end of her life, social worker in New York. Her real name was Marie Dolores Eliza Rosanna Gilbert.

Metropolitan Museum

2. What Camera Shall I Use?

WHEN you buy a camera, you plunge into a wilderness. From the $1 box camera to the $300 Contax, the name of cameras is legion. Variety is necessary; but it adds to chaos. To be sure, no one camera can do everything; but multiplicity of makes on the market makes choice difficult. Therefore, before buying a camera, analyze what kind of photographs you want to make.

Photography is the most protean of arts. It ranges from snapshots of family and friends, pets and trips, to serious scientific studies; from aerial mapping to candid shots in night clubs; from microphotography to photomurals. But photography did not come by its universal character in a mechanical manner. "Load, aim, shoot" is excellent advice for those who ask no more of photography than casual snapshots of no especial technical or esthetic merit. But if you want something more—works of art such as we find in the prints of the masters, faithful documents of personal experience, reportage of daily life—you have to define your purpose clearly and then understand what cameras and lenses are capable of doing.

My intention in this chapter is not to supply a buyers' manual of cameras and lenses. That would be a whole book in itself, and indeed an excellent reference work of this kind is the *Photographic Buyers' Handbook* (see bibliography). The August, 1939, issue of Consumers Union Reports (pp. 21-28) supplements the handbook's data, while *Popular Photography's* annual directory number each May brings it up to date. Now the import market is so unstable that it is hard to say what cameras can be obtained in the class of high grade, expensive instruments. The fine German-made machines, such as Linhof, Rolleiflex, Zeiss Juwel, Contax and Leica, have set standards for technical perfection in camera design and manufacture which will continue to control our judgment of new cameras as they come on the market. A fortunate aspect of restriction of foreign imports is that it has compelled American photographic manufacturers to enter into the production of better quality cameras, a field they should have entered long ago.

The big question is: what kind of photographs do you want to make? Will snapshots made with a simple, inexpensive box camera satisfy your creative sense? Will you never want to photograph baby in the shade of an apple tree instead of in bright sunlight, squinting at the sun? Do more difficult interiors and portraits, still on the snapshot basis, allure you? Do you want to use a camera on a tripod and become involved with flash bulbs, time exposures, more complicated calculations of shutter speed and diaphragm opening? Are you a circus fan tempted by rapid activity of acrobats in the dusky, romantic glare of gasoline torches? Does the incredibly agile motion of athletes diving, jumping, running, fascinate you, as the grace of a dancer's movement does another? Is it photography as self-expression which interests you, with the myriad subjects art may use—landscape, still life, genre, street scenes? Does human character obsess you, so that you constantly study the faces of people, trying to imagine how the visible form reveals the person beneath? Do you like to creep up on people, catch them off guard, see hidden selfs behind the masks they customarily show the world?

These questions show the wide world where photographers may adventure, according to interest and inclination. You know best why you are interested in photography. I can suggest in broad terms what camera is best suited for a given purpose. You will have to make the choice. Even the best all-purpose camera involves compromise; and you will never be wholly happy unless you accept the fact that every type of camera, and every make, has limitations. Your job is to understand your camera's potential and stretch it to the limit. But don't think that a racehorse of a camera makes a good plowhorse—or vice versa.

The old-fashioned fixed focus box camera, which does not require focusing or possess lens and shutter adjustments, is the simplest, easiest to operate and cheapest camera. The simplicity and cheapness of box cameras is the measure of their capacity for photographic achievement. Snapshots in bright light are their limit, though they are now being sold at slight extra cost with small flash reflectors. Slightly higher in complexity and cost are folding roll film cameras of the guess focus type, popularized by Kodak. With cameras of this caliber, it is possible to take pictures in shadow, early morning or late afternoon, or indoors with photofloods or flashlights. Guess focus makes it necessary, however, if one is to obtain sharp pictures, to estimate distance from lens to subject carefully. Pacing is practical, if you remember that the pace varies with individuals and that a woman's pace is shorter than a man's. Measuring the distance will save you many out-of-focus negatives.

Leaving "blind" cameras, we may consider cameras which are capable of operations of considerable flexibility and so can reproduce on light-sensitive film a latent image comparable to what the eye imagines. This is not to imply that good photographs may not be made with simpler cameras. Genthe made his masterpiece of the San Francisco fire of 1906 with a Kodak 3A he borrowed after his own professional equipment had been lost in the fire. The point is: no art, science, technic, evolved by human intelligence is worth a cent unless human mind and heart control its use. Human thought and emotion are complex and subtle, oriented not only by the individual's memory of personal experience, but also by the memory we call history. A modern flour mill may operate without a man in sight, machinery attuned to the function of grinding wheat into flour. But to suggest that machine can supplant man in the complicated interplay of ideas and feelings which is photography is a mechanical philosophy. To make photography useful, valuable, expressive, powerful, we have cameras and lenses and processes capable of adaptation to the creative intent of their user. Here we move into a broad and often highly specialized field.

How specialized we may illustrate. Are you, the reader, an architect, a lawyer, an engineer, an artist, a writer, a doctor? Then you may be working in photography because you think of it as a valuable adjunct to your profession. But each profession has to use photography in a different way. For architectural studies, a view camera with all possible swings and adjustments is needed. The painter who wants to make photographs of subjects to work up later in the studio needs a camera which can record life and action; a miniature type is suitable. The engineer who wants to record construction progress on a dam will need to use a view camera or a hand and stand camera. The lawyer who needs legal proof of the existence of documents will have recourse to a miniature camera copying outfit. The student of wild life may wish to profit by the experience of Eliot Porter (*U. S. Camera Magazine*, No. 3, March-April, 1939, pp. 18 ff.) with a small view camera. Writers will be guided by the kind of writing they do or the purpose to which their photographs are to be put. Medievalists can accelerate their studies by copying old manuscripts hidden away in provincial libraries in Europe, using for the purpose a miniature camera copying apparatus with supplementary lenses, while a novelist writing of farmers in America today can illustrate his work with documents from real life, using a hand or a hand and stand camera.

The broad use of photography as hobby, recreation or self-expression is complicated by the fact that choice of camera depends also on subject matter. The angle of those of you who like to make photographic records of other interest, as dog shows, races, sports of all kinds, differs from that of those who come to photography desiring to use its capacities as art. Again there is photo-journalism, which amateurs more and more are entering. Through great numbers and wide geographic distribution, they give a physical coverage impossible to the professional news photographer, who may or may not be lucky enough to be on the scene when the great news picture of the century breaks.

To meet these varied interests, a variety of cameras exists, more complex in structure and capable of greater complexity of function than the "blind" cameras discussed above. Among them, the serious amateur should really make his choice. Through controlled focusing of the image, interchangeable lenses, range of shutter speeds, these cameras give the photographer mechanical facilities for equating the camera eye's vision with the human eye's more imaginative and compensatory vision. With such cameras, the photographer can execute more difficult tasks—take snapshots by very poor light, at home, in the street, in the theater, without tripod or flash; make high speed action shots; do excellent pictorial work; use wide angle or long focus lenses as need. Roughly, cameras of this degree of technical development may be divided into two groups, those with ground glasses and the miniature camera of from 1 x 1 inch to 2¼ x 2¼ inches.

Ground glass cameras are equipped with a screen of semi-opaque glass at the back. This enables the photographer to see full size the image of the subject he is photographing. There are three types—view, hand and stand, and reflecting. In the view and the hand and stand types, this is made possible by the fact that the diaphragm of the lens is opened (no film being in the camera) and the photographer then can see the image on the ground glass. In cameras of the reflecting type, the image is seen by a system of mirrors and in some cases by the use of an extra lens, as in the twin reflexes Rolleiflex and Zeiss Ikoflex.

The view camera, though heavier to carry and slower to operate, has features not found in other ground glass cameras, except some of the finer quality and higher priced hand and stand cameras, like Deardorff's new Triamapro. The most important among these are the swings and the rising and falling front, which make it possible to correct vertical and horizontal distortion and at the same time to preserve depth of field. In buying a view camera, remember that adjustments are the true measure of its usefulness. The chapter on swings (Chapter 11) discusses the point at length. Another essential feature is a double or triple extension bellows so that longer focal length lenses may be used and also so that the photographer may approach his subject more closely. The cost of a view camera, about $30, has to be computed with the addition of cost of film holders, case, tripod, and battery of lenses. In my opinion, the best size is 5 x 7; for you can use a 4 x 5 reducing back if necessary, yet also make acceptable contact prints from the full sized negative.

The hand and stand camera field has been dominated till recently by the German-made Linhof and Zeiss Juwel, the former selling at $160 to $375, according to size and lens, and the latter selling at $354 in 5 x 7 size with Zeiss Tessar f/4.5 lens. The Linhof is no longer being imported, though the Juwel is said to be in stock in sufficient quantity for another year. To meet the need for a high quality, precision instrument of domestic manufacture, Deardorff began to experiment some years ago with the Triamapro. This camera has been in use for about two years but has just begun to come on the market, due to orders for defense purposes. The camera, 4 x 5 in size, sells for $165 without lenses. Its bellows extension of 19 inches, drop bed of 30 degrees (which also tilts up 15 degrees), swinging and sliding front, swinging lens board, rising and falling front, revolving back, are all features which give the camera great flexibility in the hands of an experienced operator. Comparisons aside, it is an American-made camera which should supply the facilities for high grade work. A further advantage of the camera, which it shares with other hand and stand cameras, is that it may be held in the hand and used without a tripod, if rigid support is not essential, that is, if the subject does not require use of its adjustments or if it calls for a fast shot.

Folmer Graflex's Speed Graphic, ranging in size from 3¼ x 4¼ to 5 x 7 and in price from $113.75 to $165, occupies a commanding position among hand and stand cameras. The importance of this camera, the favorite of American news photographers, and of its companion, the Graflex, may be gauged by the amount of attention paid them, as in Morgan & Lester's *Graphic Graflex Photography*. The Speed Graphic can be used for many purposes where flexible swings are not needed. A major attraction is its sturdiness and aptitude for speed. It has a ground glass for careful focusing and composition when speed is not essential, and it is also equipped with a focal range finder for rapid focusing when the film is all set for exposure. A further feature is the two type shutter system, of focal plane shutter and between-the-lens shutter. The former permits the use of high speeds up to 1/1200 second for press work; the latter works at slower speeds and is better adapted to synchronized flashlight work. The camera has a rising front, interchangeable lens board, double extension bellows, and drop bed for use with wide angle lens. The Speed Graphic is popular and widely used, not only by news photographers but by professional photographers generally and by amateurs who like to work with an eye level ground glass camera capable of making high speed action shots.

Reflecting cameras, by virtue of their construction, have the great advantage that the photographer can see his picture as he takes it, the image being reflected from a mirror onto a ground glass, viewed through a hood. They may be either of twin lens or single lens design. As is generally true throughout photography, what you gain at one point you lose at another. In the twin lens reflex camera, the ground glass image is brighter. It cannot, however, be judged as to depth of field, because the lens through which the image is seen is not the lens through which the picture is photographed; in other words, as you focus the working lens, you look at an image seen through the other lens, whose diaphragm remains wide open. With lenses of the focal length used on these cameras the factor of depth of field is not crucial, however. In general, the reflex camera is invaluable when you are photographing subjects which need to be followed around, which cannot be posed, and which are so active as to require a fairly fast shutter speed. Children and dogs, this boils down to. And why, I cannot help wondering, are the words always paired? Are there no dogs without children, or vice versa? At any rate, children and dogs do require a camera which can be held at waist level or lower, while the subject is viewed and focused on up to the instant of making the exposure. The lower height at which the reflex camera is used is an advantage, as it brings the lens into the plane of the small child or pet; and the shutter speed is fast enough to stop action. In this class, the twin lens reflex cameras, Rolleiflex and Rolleicord and Zeiss Ikoflex are all excellent. The single lens reflex cameras are led by the old standby, the Graflex, somewhat larger.

Reflex cameras have the merit that they can be aimed at a right angle to the photographer. This is particularly easy with cameras like the Rolleiflex and Ikoflex, because the photographer can still look into the hood while rotating the camera in his hands so that the lens looks off at a 90-degree angle from the direction in which he is ostensibly looking. In fact, he can even use the camera looking backwards. This kind of detective work with a camera was anticipated twenty-five years ago when Paul Strand attached a prism to his reflex camera so that the lens looked in one direction and took the picture at a right angle. Since then the prism has often been used for candid photography. But only cameras like those mentioned are so constructed as to permit this type of operation without a special adapter, except for the angle view finders on miniature cameras—which are another matter.

The miniature camera has become associated in the public mind with the 35 mm. Contax and Leica. However, cameras from 1 x 1 inch up to 2¼ x 3¼ inches may be considered miniature. The great vogue for miniature cameras has been for "candid" shots of people taken off guard or close up—A kind of photographic detective work. The popularity of this model is proved by the publication of numerous books, notable among them Morgan & Lester's *Miniature Camera Work.* (See bibliography.) The fine professional instruments, Contax and Leica, have been paid that sincerest compliment of imitation in low-priced models selling around $10. An American-made quality miniature camera, the Eastman 35 mm. Ektra, selling for $300, has now come on the market but as yet has scarcely been tested by experience. The Zeiss Tenax, size 1 x 1, selling for $60, has a special usefulness for amateurs interested in making 16 mm. motion pictures and also for motion picture workers who use these cameras to make location shots. This seems a use almost as highly specialized as the use of the Contax for photographing skin diseases—both excellent examples of the human and social value of photography, but somewhat removed from the beaten track of the millions who follow photography for fun.

A prime advantage of the miniature camera is portability, not to be sneezed at when one is traveling light. The miniature camera is unquestionably superior for night subjects because of its short focal length lens and great depth of field at wide apertures. If the night view is of a character where long exposure is possible, the argument does not hold good.

On the whole, I should advise against starting life with a miniature camera. It is an expensive, complicated machine, though capable of producing masterpieces in the hands of the expert. It requires costly accessories and expensive enlarging equipment. Furthermore, because the miniature camera demands extra care in processing, it puts a heavy burden on the photographer's craftsmanship. The perfect negatives needed to produce gratifying pictures from miniature films require that the photographer thoroughly understand lenses, exposure, problems of foscusing, processing. This basic knowledge he will acquire more easily and better on a larger camera. That is why I recommend beginning photography with a ground glass camera, preferably a view camera. But more of that in Chapter 11.

Type of work you wish to do defined and size determined, look over cameras and select one within the price range you can afford. Though the habit of swapping is bad, you can explore the secondhand market if you deal with a reputable firm and get a guarantee. At the point of actually buying a camera, a further consideration comes into play, namely, your personal relation to your camera. If you hesitate between, say, a Rolleiflex and an Ikoflex, it is probably because you feel more at home with one than with the other. This may be illogical. Nevertheless, these affinities are like friendships; you click with some people and not with others. You may feel more at ease with the mechanism or handling of one camera than of another. Other things being equal, that is the camera for you. For example, mechanically minded people will like a camera, the complexity of whose design and operation estranges another kind of person. Even the placement of buttons and levers involves tiny but important psychological factors. Here personal taste decides, as it does between chocolate and vanilla.

4. BOATING ON THE HUDSON — Margaret Bourke-White

Life Magazine

5. HINDENBURG DISASTER

Amateurs give a wide news coverage for unpredictable events such as the Hindenburg explosion.

Pictures Inc.

3. What Else Do I Need?

GADGETLAND is America's happy hunting ground. In photography, the American dream is that if you only have enough accessories, appurtenances, and devices, the machine will take care of the picture. Of course, this isn't true. It's still the man (don't forget the woman!) behind the camera that counts. Nevertheless, a minimum of indispensable equipment is required.

Carrying Cases

A camera case is essential for convenience in carrying and for protection, type varying according to camera. Small cameras come with neat leather cases, to be slung by strap over the shoulder. Height of luxury is the custom-built case, with plush-padded compartments for each item of equipment. When the camera is carried separately, accessories are best tucked in a pocket which will button or close with a zipper. Otherwise, the instant you bend over, out fall exposure meter and all; and repair bills can be enormous. Likewise, if small cameras are carried in a pocket, they should be buttoned or zipped in. For view cameras, the standard case provides space for camera, a dozen film holders, focusing cloth, exposure meter and other necessities. If you are not athletically disposed, divide the load in two parts, carrying the camera in one case and film holders, etc., in another.

Tripods

The problem of tripods is still to be solved. Ideally, a tripod should be sturdy and rigid, able to resist gales and hurricanes, and weigh one ounce, as well as folding to vest pocket size. Instead, tripods are big, clumsy to carry, heavy and generally unsatisfactory. Nevertheless, you have to have one. Too often the photographer selects a very light tripod in order to save on weight and space; but a flimsy tripod which shakes with every breeze is worse than no tripod at all. The first "must" is rigidity. As cameras need to be flexible yet simple in operation, so do tripods. A two-way tilting head is desirable because the camera may have to be tipped sidewise as well as backward and forward, as it is not always used straight on but sometimes aimed from unusual angles. In such cases, it is simpler to tilt the tripod top than to shorten a leg of the tripod. To level off the tripod when it is set up on uneven ground, it is easier to tilt the top than to make an adjustment of the legs. The tripod must be adapted to your camera. With drop-bed cameras, like the Deardorff Triamapro, Linhof and Speed Graphic, the tripod head must be small enough to allow the bed to drop freely. Frequently this means that an adapter has to be added to your accessories.

For smaller cameras, as Contax and Ikonta or even Rolleiflex and Graflex, a chain tripod will stop the hand's quivering. In most cases, it helps obtain a sharp image, especially at the slower speeds from 1/5 to 1/50 of a second. The Zeiss chain tripod is excellent; and the six-inch rigid tubular handle which stores the chain when not in use can act as a firm handle for the camera as well. The chain tripod has the advantage of light weight and compactness. If you do not wish to spend several dollars for a chain tripod, you can devise an acceptable substitute by fitting into your hand camera a large-headed short screw, to which a length of heavy twine is then fastened. Use twine which will not stretch or break easily, black fishline being best for the purpose.

Sunshades

The type of sunshade you buy will be determined by the camera you own. But make no mistake, a sunshade is not a gadget, it is a necessity. In ninety per cent of photographs, the result is vastly improved by using a sunshade, even if there is no direct danger of halation.

Filters

I think that the arguments for filters are exaggerated; and unless you are thoroughly familiar with their use, I advise using only one or at most two. A medium yellow for orthochromatic film and a medium yellow-green for panchromatic, which fits the lens snugly, are all that are really needed to begin with. In advising against too many filters, I repeat a basic conviction: the secret of photography is to simplify! Photography is a highly specialized body of knowledge, and its intricacies must be mastered if one is to have the fullest success. But there can be complication of method and means which serves no good end.

Filters, I believe, have been misused. There has been a tendency in contemporary photography to overdramatize skies. They are made stormy, turbulent, dark, romantic, with tonal contrasts between the blue of the sky and the white of clouds which are far more emphatic than in nature. Many good sky effects have been photographed by taking the picture early in the morning or late in the afternoon. Since natural light is less yellow at midday, at that time a filter may be used to hold back strong blue and ultraviolet rays in sunlight, which would otherwise overexpose your sky or similar bright subjects (snow, white sails, reflected light from ocean or lake) and so fail to reproduce the tonal difference between blue and white as registered by the eye. A further argument against indiscriminate use of filters is that they increase length of exposure. If short exposures are necessary for the type of work you do, this is a definite handicap.

Focusing Cloths

A focusing cloth is a necessity, in my opinion, not only with view cameras but also with ground glass cameras which have leather hoods. I believe, after looking at hundreds of students' prints, that most photographers only half *see* their pictures. Unless you carefully move your eyes opposite each corner of the ground glass and note every area, you will see only the center of the ground glass. This is done with considerable strain even if you have first-class eyesight. Since the head has to be held a foot away to permit the eyes to focus, it is plain that extraneous light must be shut out so that the image seen on the ground glass may be bright and sharp.

To see all parts of the image critically, use a focusing cloth. The rubber ones crack and admit light. Nor is a skimpy black cloth sufficient—or efficient. The focusing cloth should be completely opaque, even if this entails sewing two together so that they are of double thickness. In very hot climates, it may be advisable to use (as Edward Weston does) a focusing cloth of which the outside layer is white to reflect the sun's heat. With cameras like the Rolleiflex, equipped with short leather hoods, there is too much intercepting light when the eyes are held the proper distance from the ground glass. Focusing is facilitated by slipping a longer hood over the one already attached to the camera.

All this, of course, assuming that you really want to see your image, which implies in turn that you are determined to make the most of photography. Seeing the picture before you take it is insurance against disappointment. From the beginning you have taken control and mean to plan your photograph. When you have reached this psychological attitude toward photography, you have reached the stage people are always emphasizing, the purposive function of the man behind the camera.

Lens Caps

Consistent use of lens caps to protect your lenses if they are removable is a wise precaution, as you will learn from bitter experience if you have to have lenses reground because of careless handling. Further care of the lens—as well as a necessary step to insure negatives free from dust spots —is to clean it before using. Lens tissue is another "must" of your pack kit, though a fine old *linen* handkerchief is better because it does not leave specks or fiber on the lens. A brush to dust out parts of the camera particularly open to dust or soot is also needed.

Cable Releases

Cable releases are practically indispensable, so if they do not come with your camera, invest in them. Their function is to prevent jarring the camera when you "press the button." They also permit you to stand aside (if the camera is being used on a tripod) and study the effect the instant before you click the shutter. This is particularly important in taking portraits, because human expression is fleeting and the photographer has to be ready, cable release in hand, to catch the characteristic look.

6. SAN FRANCISCO FIRE, 1906 — ARNOLD GENTHE

Taken with a 3A Kodak.

7. TIME OUT FOR BEER — Berenice Abbott

Taken with Rolleiflex; 1/100 second; f/22; 2 flash bulbs.

Courtesy Fortune Magazine and P. Ballantine & Sons

Spirit Levels

For all cameras used on a tripod, it is essential to level off the camera, otherwise the photograph may be tilted. A slanting horizon line can spoil an otherwise good shot. Many cameras today come with built-in levels. Small good quality carpenter's levels, costing about 50 cents in a hardware store, do the trick admirably and save you many heartaches for fine pictures gone askew.

Exposure Meters

The question of exposure meters is complicated. Their usefulness is not in dispute, only the degree of perfection which has been attained in design and manufacture. Of meters of professional quality, both Weston and General Electric score high. The detailed technical analysis of *Photographic Buyers' Handbook* may be used for guidance in this field, as well as the July, 1940, issue of Consumers' Union Reports, pp. 7-9.

In taking photographs, the exposure meter gives a precise measurement, which becomes one factor in the equation of shutter speed, size of diaphragm opening, film speed and character of subject. There is no doubt photography needs precise measurements at every step for fullest effectiveness. It was a great advance in photographic method when Hurter and Driffield in 1890 made the experiments on which time and temperature development is based. Collateral advance in printing has not yet taken place, though mass production photofinishing plants use the photoelectric cell to measure the density of negatives and so mechanically to calculate exposure time for prints. The development of an instrument for measuring intensity of light, similarly, was a great step forward in method at the initial and crucial stage of photography, making the negative. But I personally should like to see exposure meters even more sensitive and accurate and certainly less susceptible to deterioration or physical injury than at present.

Exposure itself is discussed in Chapter 13. Here I want simply to stress the importance of correctly measuring light and of relating this factor to film speed, which then determines size of aperture and length of exposure in relation to all other factors, as activity of moving objects, etc. When you use your meter—whatever model you supply yourself with, Weston or

General Electric, or one of the less expensive makes—remember one thing: film speed ratings are based on ideal conditions. In using them with exposure meter readings, you have to be something of a pessimist and overestimate the time needed; otherwise you will find your negatives badly underexposed. Reliable exposures can be read from the *Wellcome Calculator*, price 90 cents, or the *Quick-Set*, price $1.

Film

In discussing equipment and accessories, we should not overlook film. Naturally you use film according to what your camera requires—roll film for roll film cameras, film packs if your camera will take only film pack, cut film for view cameras. But, in buying a camera, I would be guided to an extent by what facilities it offered as far as film is concerned. For example, between two cameras of about equal merits, one of which took a simple roll film and the other of which required special magazines, I should prefer the one easier to load. On the other hand, between film pack and cut film, I should vote for the latter, because it is cheaper, more rigid and offers a greater variety of types of emulsion. These advantages seem to me to outweigh the trouble of loading film holders.

Actually, the bugbear of loading film has been exaggerated. The procedure is fairly simple, once you understand it and establish a good habitual routine. In fact, I want to emphasize that the secret of being successful in photography is to create good habits of workmanship as you go along. Photography is not casual, accidental. It requires as much care and forethought as good technicians exercise in a laboratory. Cut film must be loaded in the darkroom. Some cameras supply two or three film holders; but you will need at least six, preferably more. First, practice loading in bright light with old negatives or paper cut to size. When you load the virgin film, it should be in total darkness. The sensitive (dull) side must be loaded face up, toward the outside of the holder. Notches cut in the film guide the worker in the dark. When the notches (designating type of film) are in the upper right-hand corner, the face of the film is on top. Be sure that the silver edge of the slide holder also faces outward. After you have exposed the film, you must replace the slide with its black edge outward, as a warning that the film has been used.

Choice of film lies between orthochromatic and panchromatic. The arguments for orthochromatic film are: it is cheaper, of finer grain, with thinner emulsion to give sharper images, and can be developed under a safelight, whereas panchromatic film, being more sensitive, generally needs to be developed in complete darkness. The arguments in favor of panchromatic film have to do with esthetic factors: its tonalities are more subtle and truer to life for the most part, though red may sometimes appear too light, and it is faster than orthochromatic film. In the slower speed panchromatic films, emulsion is also thin and gives the desired sharp image. Weighing these qualities, the choice boils down to a personal one. Panchromatic film is more sensitive to all colors, hence the prefix "pan," while orthochromatic is sensitive to most colors except red, so that in a print from orthochromatic film red appears dark. In the photograph of Heymann's butcher shop, I had to use orthochromatic film so that the red-lettered signs would strike the eye with all their natural impact of harshness and blatancy. Orthochromatic film is good for portraits, especially of men and children, though women's makeup photographs too dark.

A further consideration is the type of enlarger you use. Orthochromatic film is suitable for enlargers with diffused light, while panchromatic is good for the condenser type, which otherwise is likely to give too "contrasty" prints. If you do not enlarge, this factor is negligible. As to the word contrasty, a note may be added; for its use is confusing. Perhaps the best definition is that in *Basic Photography*.

Briefly, it may be defined as meaning that the range between black and white is greater and more apparent than in so-called "normal" negatives or prints. There are fewer intermediate tones between black and white; therefore the "contrast" seems sharper and harsher. Usually, extreme contrast is to be avoided. The choice between panchromatic and orthochromatic will be partly determined by this fact.

As to what make of film shall be bought, "it matters little" (writes A. R. Lambert in *Photographic Buyers' Handbook*, p. 137) "whether *Agfa*, *Eastman* or *Defender* film is used. Equally good results (and equally bad ones) can be obtained with the products of any of the major film-manufacturers." The statement applies to casual snapshots. In the realm of professional photographers or expert amateurs, differences begin to emerge, and experience then becomes the best guide.

4. A Point of View

NOW that you've chosen a camera, let's go outdoors and take pictures. First, organize your field trip. Photography is more fun if you don't start out on expeditions with half your equipment missing or in bad repair. Check sunshade, filters, spirit levels, lens tissue and brush, cable releases, exposure meter, whatever accessories you need for your camera—are they all safely stowed away in the camera case? Above all, don't take along unnecessary packages. If the trip is to be made by car, do not set the camera on the floor; even the best shock absorbers will not take up all the vibrations which can damage a camera's delicate construction.

Comfortable clothes with many pockets are certainly desirable. Women, wear small hats, and don't carry handbags! Keep your hands and arms free for work. If the weather is cold, wear warmer clothes than usual. You'll be surprised how cold you get, standing around while you unlimber camera and tripod, focus it and all.

The question is; what shall I photograph? The answer was partly decided long ago—at least as long ago as Chapter 2, in which we discussed various interests in photography and the sort of camera needed on the basis of the sort of photographs you want to make. But there is one thing you can count on in photography, the unpredictable. You may start out to photograph babies and dogs and find suddenly that the only thing in the world you want to photograph is apple trees in blossom. Or you may begin with portraits of human beings and turn to portraits of buildings. The important thing is what *you* see and how simply and directly you see it. So I want to discuss a point of view for photography.

Learn to see the world as it is, I have called this point of view. Others might call it "straight" photography, or "documentary," or "realistic." Whatever it is called, the first step is to see through your own eyes, not by the memory of what others have seen. Many wax ecstatic over faraway subjects. But you need not go far from home to find themes. Your own community, your own backyard, contain valuable material. Some of our most common American scenes look weird and fascinating to foreign visitors—as tattooed Africans do to us. In the end, you will find greater happiness in photography if you study familiar scenes and activities around you, the things you know best. Subjects you know inside out from daily personal association give photographs greater originality and authority than casual, hasty snapshots of subjects, the "feel" of which you cannot convey from lack of knowledge. There is no need to imitate the photographs of other photographers; let your own intimate knowledge of homely, living themes speak for itself.

What if you live in the country? Farm animals are always fascinating, as is farm machinery and farm architecture. Animals can be seen in many moods—moods of comedy, of dignity, of tragedy, even, or (as Walt Whitman saw them) "placid and self-contain'd." There are roads wandering over hillsides, and the vast sweep of prairie lands. There are bridges, and people working. There are bright clouds, and children playing. There is the other side of life, also, the darker side which has been recorded with great human sympathy by the Farm Security Administration photographers—the ravages of soil erosion and "dust bowl," the migration of disinherited farmers. In *An American Exodus,* Dorothea Lange and Paul S. Taylor have presented a moving and beautiful "record of human erosion." A document of such subject matter is Russell Lee's photograph, here shown, of an old woman's gnarled hands, which states powerfully yet simply the beauty, the tears, of old age and toil.

The active life of village or town has a vast panorama of human interest. The people you know, the things they do habitually, important houses and buildings in the community, streets and their activity, events of daily occurrence, are good photographic material. How such seemingly humdrum subject matter may be developed is indicated by such photo stories as Margaret Bourke-White's classic on "Middletown" (Muncie, Indiana) in *Life* some years ago, or another photo feature of *Life* on the Pelham (Mass.) town meeting. Even more ambitious in its scope is J. W. McManigal's photographic essay in *U. S. Camera Annual,* 1941, vol. 1, "Horton, Kansas—A Midland Chronicle."

If you photograph in a big city, the situation is more complicated technically. In many cases, traffic presents an almost insuperable obstacle. It is often impossible to set up the tripod where you want to, or even to stand still for a few moments with a hand camera. Imagine photographing Times Square on Election Night from ground level! To capture the spirit of the modern city with hurrying crowds, congested traffic, skyscrapers, the photographer has to create points of view quite different from the traditional eye-level vantage point of old-fashioned picture-making like easel painting. Angle shots imported from the movies, birds'-eye views, worms'-eye views, rooftop views, are all part of the complete envisioning of the city's complex architectural stratifications. The photographer may have to shoot from a window or a roof. The height at which to take the photograph is important for "drawing," and brings up interesting esthetic considerations. Paradoxically, some views look best from the safe and sane sidewalk, so that uninteresting roofs are eliminated from the view. It is a significant comment on the lack of city planning in the United States that New York presents a tremendous problem in photography. The sharp contrasts between the skyscrapers and the brownstone fronts intensifies chaos; the culture morphology of New York shows sharp antagonisms in form, an anarchic heterogeneity. Atget, in photographing Paris, at least had the advantage of a subject of relative homogeneity.

Wherever you work, you follow the same general procedure. Beyond the mechanics of taking the picture lies the great zone where intelligence, imagination, will, combine to create the photographer's choice. Rules which will help you in learning to make that choice are given in a shorthand form:

1. Choose your subject—landscape, city scene, person, pet or what.
2. Study your subject for the best angle of view. If possible, walk all around it.
3. Choose your perspective, by walking closer to and farther away from your subject.
4. Decide on the height of camera, whether ground level, waist level, eye level or higher.
5. Decide on the center of interest, so that it controls your picture as you see it in ground glass or finder.
6. Examine the foreground for details to enhance the photograph.

8. HEYMANN'S BUTCHER SHOP — Berenice Abbott

Superplenachrome film was used to make red letters dark as explained in text.

9. PARIS WITHOUT SIGNS — Photographer unknown

In the days of the Third Empire, signs were not permitted in Paris, so that the early photographer of this shot had no problem as far as registering tones was concerned. Optics created another problem, as explained in the text.

10. STATUE OF LIBERTY — Berenice Abbott

How your subject will look if you walk all around it to get another point of view; taken with Rolleiflex.

11. MICHIGAN PATRIARCH — WILLIAM VANDIVERT

Taken with 3¼ x 4¼ Linhof camera; ½ second for open flash; f/32; two No. 20 flash bulbs on separate reflectors; daylight from front window; Schneider Angulon f/6.89 cm. lens; Agfa Superpan Press.

Life Magazine

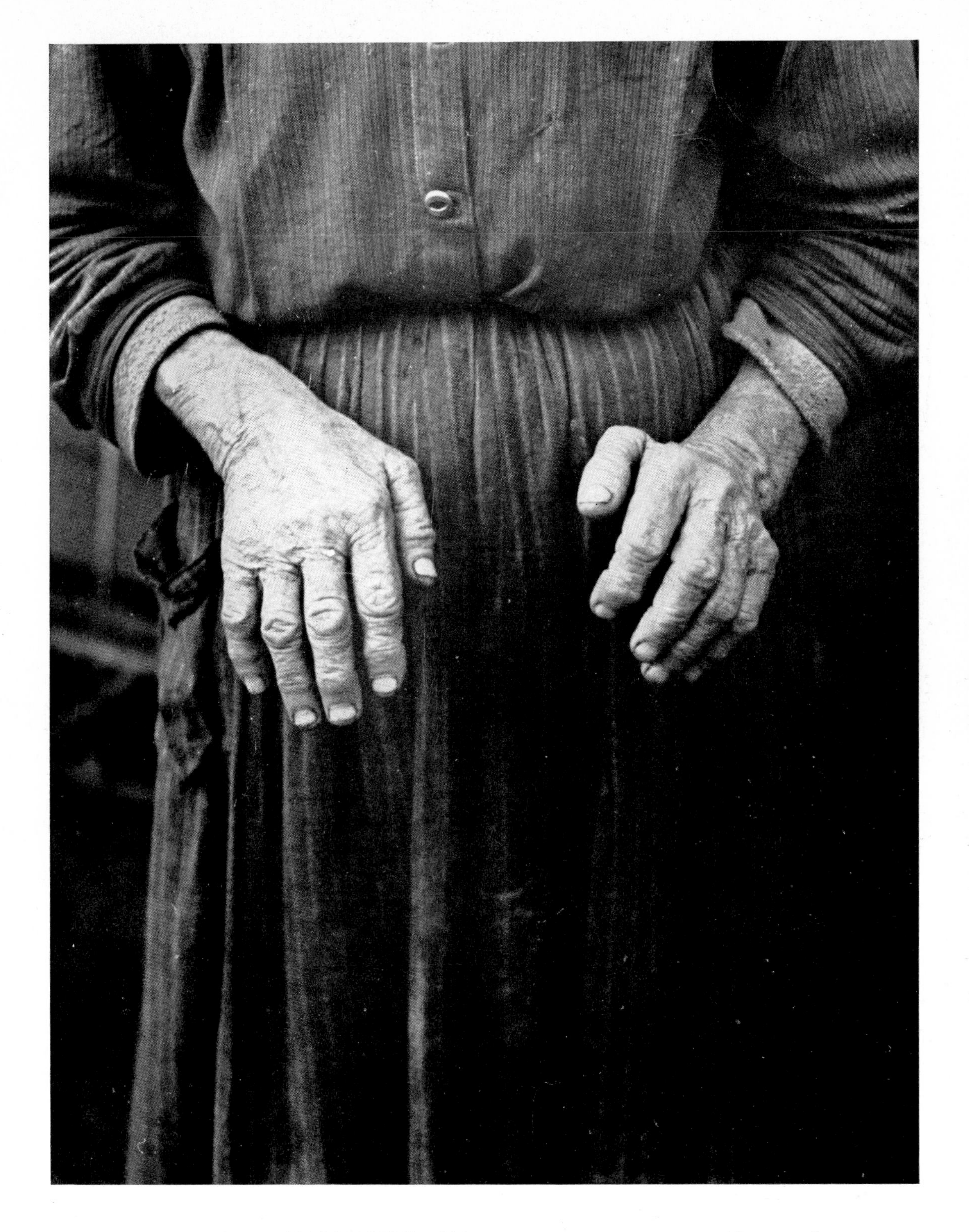

12. OLD WOMAN'S HANDS, 1936 RUSSELL LEE

"The hands are those of a pioneer, one who came from Europe and settled in Iowa on a farm." Contax; 5 cm. lens; Panatomic.

Courtesy of the Farm Security Administration

13. STOCK EXCHANGE: I — BERENICE ABBOTT

8 x 10 Century Universal view camera.

14. STOCK EXCHANGE: II — BERENICE ABBOTT

8 x 10 Century Universal view camera; 1/50 second; f/11.

15. FLAGELLATION — BARBARA MORGAN

Taken with 4 x 5 Speed Graphic; 1/700 second; f/11; Agfa Triple S cut film; Agfa 17 developer.

Erick Hawkins in *El Penitente*, in which he danced with Martha Graham and Merce Cunningham. Highly specialized photography such as this requires that the photographer carry his idea through from the moment of exposure till the final print is made.

7. Compose the principal subject in relation to background, whether contrasting buildings, clouds, hills, water, earth.

8. Regulate the sharpness of background and foreground in relation to the central theme. Don't let the foreground be fuzzy.

9. Be sure the sun does not strike the lens or the front of the camera. Remember the sunshade.

10. If the light is flat and uninteresting, take the photograph at another time of day.

11. Study the image on the ground glass, and apply what you know of composition and lighting.

12. When calculating exposure, think how the subject will look in the final print. Then expose to obtain detail in the necessary shadows.

13. Keep notes on exposure, time of day, film, etc., and you will learn even from failures.

14. If more than a third of the picture is sky or white objects (buildings, signs, statues, horses) against a blue sky, place a medium yellow or yellow green filter over the lens and increase time of exposure by the given filter factor.

15. Guard against strong winds or vibrations which may shake the camera at the instant of exposure.

16. If the print fails to meet your hopes, do the subject over, trying to correct your mistakes.

Many technical problems have to be solved when photographing outdoors. If shutter speed is too slow to stop the action of a rapidly moving figure, the photograph will show blur in the central subject. To "freeze" motion, a short exposure must be used with fast lens and film. Or, again, blur may be due to the fact that the camera has moved in the photographer's hands; for most people cannot hold a camera steady for longer than 1/50 of a second exposure. The indispensability of a tripod for high quality work may be judged by comparing two photographs taken under identical conditions, except that in one the camera is held in the hands and in the other it is set on a tripod.

If Point 9 is ignored, results will be distressing; for when direct light strikes the lens, general over-all "fogging" of the negative takes place. Always use a sunshade on the lens except when the camera's rising front has been raised to such a height that the shade might cut off corners of the film.

In that case, if there is danger of sunlight striking the lens, protect the lens with a hat or film holder slide.

A mistake photographers often make is to tilt the camera, which gives the picture a topsy-turvy appearance. To salvage such a negative, it is sometimes possible to straighten up the vertical and horizontal parallels but in so doing important parts may have to be cut into. The best system is to work with a ground glass camera so that you can see in advance what your picture looks like and correct in advance any askew, tilted lines. The spirit level comes in handy here, too. The ground glass also helps guard against sun striking the lens, for the dazzling effect can be seen at once when the image is studied.

What Makes a Good Photograph?

First of all, the good photograph is sharp. Careless focusing is fatal, especially when we think of the photographic medium's esthetic character—its neat, precise quality. Don't focus sharply on the background, when your dominant theme lies in a central plane. It is better, but not perfect, when the main theme is in focus and the background out of focus. A smaller lens opening often will bring both planes into focus, if this is desirable and if it is not necessary to stop action.

Natural light outdoors is tricky business. Though midday sun is more intense, it is likely to be flat and dull. Early morning and late afternoon light gives interesting effects; for at these times, shadows are longer and light is yellower, facts which produce tonal quality in the print. A flat, front lighting is rarely advisable. Don't photograph the main part of your picture in shadow if you can help it. Watch familiar views with the sun's rays striking across them at different angles and train your eye to differentiate effects. Study different prints of your own negatives or other photographers' and note how the lighting might have been improved. By studying the direction of the sun, you learn to foretell the time when the sun will be in the best position to photograph a given subject; for the same subject seen even half an hour apart often presents entirely different aspects. In one view the slanting rays of the sun may cast shadows which bring the whole subject to life, while in the other the theme appears dull and lifeless. Almost any scene, no matter how prosaic outwardly, may be photographed as an exciting and dramatic experience if the photographer has imagination.

Working with a plan saves time and energy, as well as money. Before going out on a Sunday afternoon photographic expedition, you will be wise to plan a bit—unless you are of that buoyant, happy-go-lucky temperament which loves the unknown for its own sake. No doubt at one time or another you have thought of many subjects you'd like to photograph. You may have made notes of them on old letters and telephone bills. Look them over and see what rough blueprint emerges. It will save time and anguish, if you are a passionate photographer who cannot bear to waste a second of the hours spent in the field. One advantage of this system is that when you saw subjects which aroused your interest to the extent that you noted them down, then you probably registered a mental note of the time of day for best lighting. Planning on a big scale will even include looking over the subject beforehand, if it is not too far away, and thinking how you want it to look in the finished photograph. As time goes on, you will be delighted at the success you have with photographs about which you thought and planned in advance.

A little story proves the point. The two photographs of the New York Stock Exchange (Plates 13 and 14) show how much better a photograph can be with study and thought. I decided to photograph the Stock Exchange in 1933. At that time, film was much slower than now; traffic, however, was as congested and rapid. Because light is none too good in the downtown cañons, I decided to take the photograph on a Sunday. But the result (*Stock Exchange: 1*) was disappointing. Human activity, flow of crowds in the narrow street, was needed to offset that static neoclassic facade. Most of all, of course, the Stock Market without feverish human movement is totally uncharacteristic. Therefore the picture had to be taken on a weekday. Moreover, for satisfactory lighting, it had to be taken at a different time of day. Then the front of the building seemed empty and blank. The American flag, I thought, would look well on that pediment, it would enhance the composition.

I had to do considerable preparation to coordinate all the elements I wanted—crowds in the street, good lighting, American flag. It developed that the flag is flown only on holidays. But—holidays are like Sundays: there are no people in the financial district, and human activity had become an essential motif in my hoped-for picture. Then began a correspondence with Richard Whitney, at that time president of the Stock Exchange, to persuade him to issue orders that the flag should be flown on a given bright morning at a certain hour. Light changes far more rapidly than you imagine, and in this case by the time the flag had been raised the light effect which struck the building only for twenty minutes was gone! The whole job had to be done over another day. Finally I "got" *Stock Exchange: 2,* which became a sort of semiofficial portrait. Certainly, no "accident" produced this photograph.

However though planning and forethought are eminently desirable, there is no law to prevent the photographer from photographing what spontaneously pleases his eye. Indeed, if plan and spontaneity can be fused in one photograph, that is the essence of photography's impact. Photography is essentially a visual medium—as Balzac said, "Sight is insight"—and if you prefer to see your picture as it happens, that is the right approach for you.

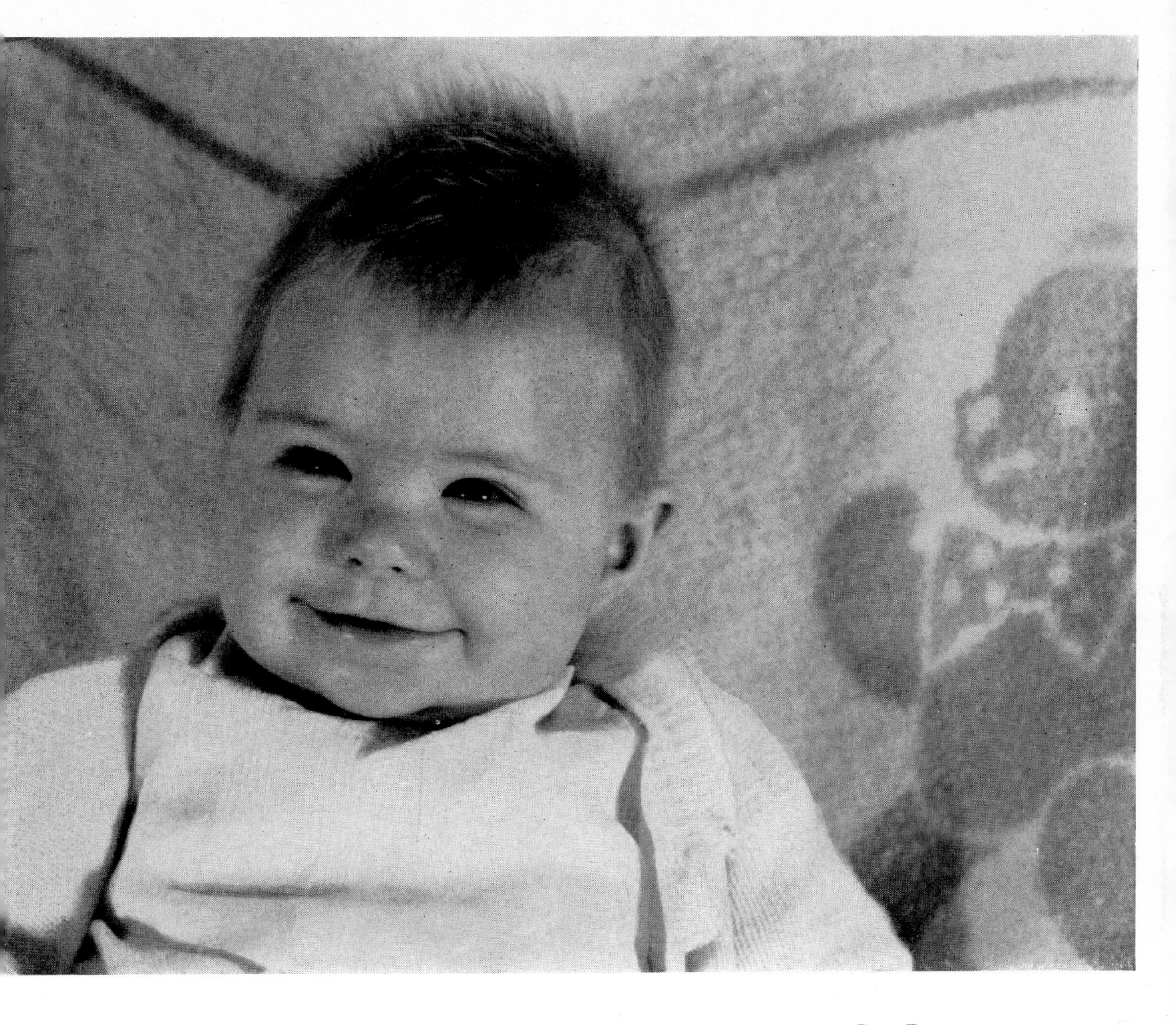

16. BABY — Gay Dillon

Taken with 4 x 5 Speed Graphic; Zeiss Tessar 5¼ inch lens; 1/50 second; f/12.5; two photofloods; camera on tripod; Eastman Super XX film pack.

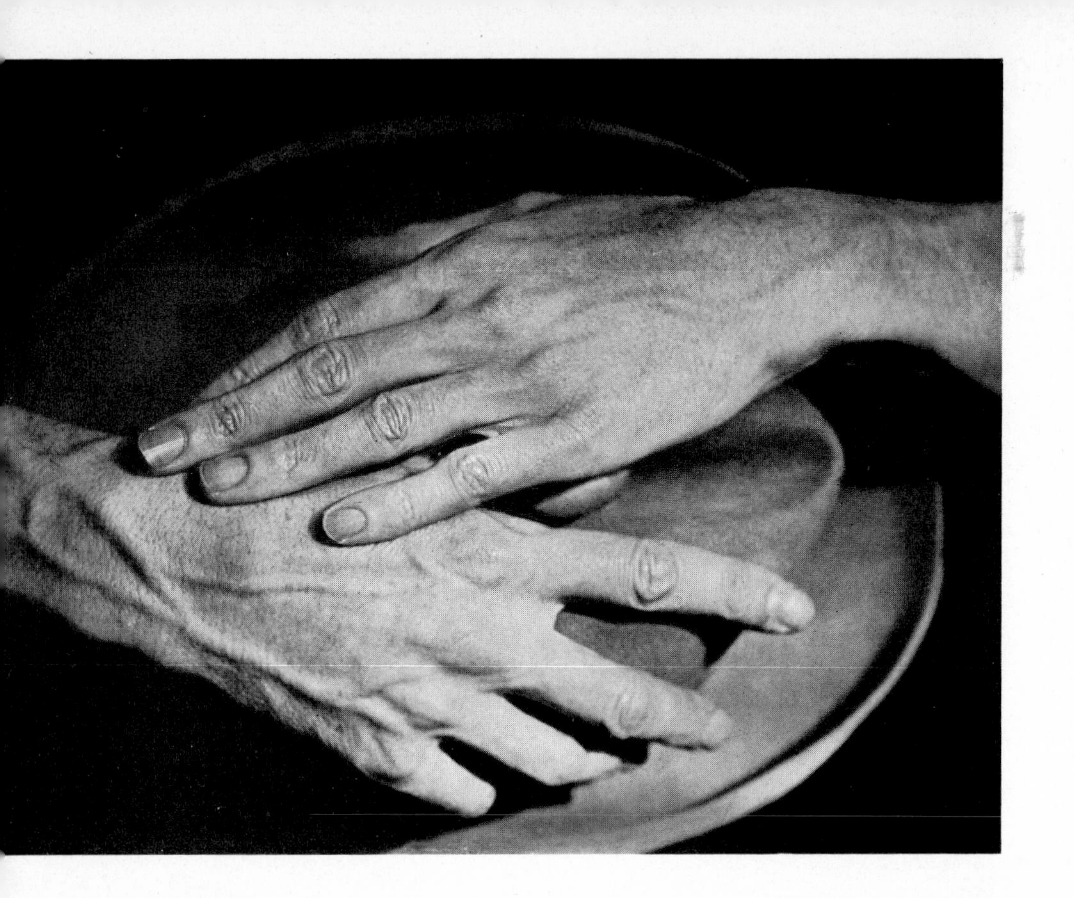

17*a*. HANDS OF JEAN COCTEAU

BERENICE ABBOTT

Taken with 9 x 12 cm. view camera, 6½ x 9 cm. reducing back, by daylight.

17*b*. BUDDY BERENICE ABBOTT

Taken with 9 x 12 cm. view camera. Posed action.

5. Do Your Own Processing

SHALL I do my own developing and printing? Emphatically, the answer is yes. This is written with no unfriendliness toward the photofinishing industry, which in New York alone can turn out upward of half a million prints a day. But the goal the serious amateur sets himself is something else. It combines the immediate pleasure in all photography's manual operations—comparable with the painter's joy in the feel of paint going on the canvas or the sculptor's exhilaration as tough wood yields to tool—with a stubborn determination to make the picture his own in every sense.

Though the perfectionist's minute splitting of esthetics is to be avoided, nevertheless the goal of perfection which the amateur sets himself is not a thing to be scorned. Rather, it represents the attitude of the photographer who works for love, unharassed by editor's deadline, not restricted by commercial assignment. First of all, the audience of the amateur is himself. It may widen, according to the merit and content of his work. But primarily he works to please himself. He succeeds best in fulfilling his purpose when he is the master of every step in the process.

What you find out as you explore the possibilities of photography is that your own criticism of your work becomes more exacting. You look at prints you made last year. "Yes, they're pretty good. The idea was good. But if I had gotten greater depth of field, then it would really have clicked." Or, "What a lousy print! Guess I had better work with that negative some more."

Your criteria have been evolving all these months and years you have been making photographs. At the same time, you have been evolving a method to produce the kind of pictures you want. This method starts when you take the picture; it involves the way you see your subject, the way you analyze light, action and exposure, the way you set up your camera, the way you choose your angle of view. Here already your knowledge is seeking to control what you do. In other words, you want to choose and select material from nature—all the real objects and activities about you—and organize it into significant expression. It is your own emotion about these things and your own ideas about them that you want to express in your finished picture.

This drive which inspires you through all the heartaches and drudgery is a genuinely creative feeling. Yet it can be thwarted by the fact that photography is still a loosely defined and coordinated art. The first premise to accept is that in photography, as in any other medium of expression or communication, you have to think your idea through. Despite the fact that you press a button and get an image, photography is the least mechanical of mediums. When you plan composition, exposure and all, you have to imagine how the subject will look after development and printing. No one else can know what mental picture you had when you pressed the button. Materialization of concept into visual expression includes the whole sequence of operations from taking the picture to printing it.

To make the photograph from beginning to end is an obligation the conscious photographer cannot escape, because he sees his picture from beginning to end and is not satisfied with less than he imagined. If conditions forbid your doing your own developing and printing, then you will get a compromise, providing the photofinisher is mechanically efficient. If you are pursuing photography as a recreation, a hobby, an outlet for your creative impulses, you'll probably never put up with such frustration. Somehow, some way, you'll find space and time for developing and printing. Why? Because half the fun of photography is fooling around, mixing solutions, playing with papers, exercising tangible authority over the silent partners of photography—film, paper, chemicals.

Indeed, the pleasure photography gives is a crescendo. There is the healthy excitement of taking the picture, of browsing around in strange quarters of a city, of prowling about water front or railroad yards, of snapping intimate genre scenes in little restaurants or shooting people's funny faces on a bus. Then there is the thrill you get from a good negative, when everything has gone right and the film is clean, transparent, properly balanced in density of darks and lights. But the great thrill of photography is making the print, when the picture finally appears in black and white, that enchanting vision you saw with your mind's eye as you pressed the button. Here is the visualization toward which you have been working. It is complete proof that photography is not automatic writing, but the creation of man's hopes and dreams and skill and will.

Glamor and romance aside, there are practical reasons why you should do your own developing and printing. In developing, you will find that you make an adjustment between the manufacturer's time and temperature instructions to suit your own particular way of making exposures. In printing, you will be able to make legitimate corrections, such as dodging, coccining, spotting, retouching, which correct inadequacies of the negative or defects in materials. (These methods are explained in later chapters.) For despite the great care taken in the manufacture of film, as described in Chapter 12, apparently there will always be pinholes and such, and even the most rigid purism would not argue against such a correction.

To become your own photofinisher involves one of two things: either you have a flair for science or you triumph by persistence over a non-scientific habit of mind. Great photographers are not necessarily born laboratory workers; but for the most expressive photography, they adopt the scientific attitude to the extent of understanding integral relations between their medium's materials and methods. Photography is still so young that scientists have not yet solved the mystery of what happens when light strikes the sensitive silver salts. Although the medium has made great strides during its century of life, it still has to cope with a number of unstable factors, one of which is the unequal results from different lots of film. Surprising and freak accidents may occur, because of this variable factor. Therefore, we must use the utmost care and precision in dealing with facts as far as we know them.

What step in photography is the most important? In the last analysis, each and every step. However, first we have our tools, then we learn to use them properly. Like any creative work, whether a novel, a piece of sculpture, a drama, the whole must be good. Likewise, each part must be complete in itself. And, finally, all the parts must fit together in an harmonious entity. With the photograph, the whole is the finished print. To obtain a final expression which is satisfying and successful, we must travel far, pass through many stages. We have camera, lens, shutter, film. Then we make use of these tools with brains, eyes, emotions, institutions, alertness, dexterity. But at any point, the whole sequence may break down if we do not understand and respect the character of the process.

Truly, if the lens is the camera eye, then chemistry is photography's heart. In chemical interactions lie the energy, the active pulse beat, to bring the latent image to life and to turn invisible into visible reality. Chemistry is no blind accident or miracle, but a complicated science. The chemical actions in photography consequently must be understood, mastered, and applied. Here accuracy in the laboratory, precision, exact weights, and correct temperatures, purity of chemicals, proper storage, are all imperative.

Of the millions of Americans who make photographs today, it is impossible to say what proportion do their own developing and printing. Certainly there are thousands and hundreds of thousands, perhaps millions. At any rate, when you have passed beyond the casual snapshot stage of photography, the chances are ten to one that you will get as much pleasure from finishing your pictures as from taking them. For my part, I cannot imagine the serious amateur's turning over a negative to a photofinisher. The commercial photographic worker, speeded up by the factory processing of thousands of films and prints in a day, cannot know or care what particular effect you desire. Yet in this hoped-for effect lies the specific meaning of the subject as you saw it. A fine conception for a picture, translated by your thought and action into a good negative, may still produce an insignificant print if improperly handled. Hence the need for every serious photographer to be his own craftsman-technician.

6. Planning Your Darkroom

THE great problem in doing your own developing and printing is to find adequate working space. Many ardent amateurs are forced back on improvisation for a darkroom, taking temporary root in bathroom, kitchen or closet, as is feasible. More fortunate are those who live spaciously in quarters boasting attics or cellars where darkrooms may be set up permanently. If space is available for a permanent darkroom to be established (contrary to the Arabs-that-folded-their-tents-in-the-night character of the improvised darkroom in bathroom or kitchen) the darkroom may be planned along ideal lines, desire and funds permitting. If it is out of the question to arrange any kind of darkroom in your home, then you will have to fall back on facilities offered by camera clubs, schools, church clubs, museums, etc.

First of all, a darkroom must be dark. Lighttightness is essential, whether you work in darkroom, kitchen, closet, or ideal photographic laboratory with Greek key lighttrap entrance. A simple test for lighttightness is described in Chapter 9. The second "must" has to do with physical facilities, i.e., running water (preferably hot as well as cold) and safely insulated electrical outlets. Ideally, the darkroom should be air-conditioned. Ideally, also, it should be in two parts: darkroom (or "wet" laboratory) and finishing room, with dry, cool storage space in the latter for negative materials, photographic papers and dry chemicals. *Basic Photography* describes standard professional specifications for a photographic workshop. A somewhat simpler description is given in Ansel Adams' *Making a Photograph.*

Cleanliness is imperative in the darkroom. Therefore its physical construction, as far as your circumstances permit, should be such as to permit easy maintenance for cleanliness. There should be ample storage shelf space; but to avoid accumulation of dust, use enclosed cabinets wherever possible, such as come in standard units for modern kitchens or for medical supplies. Otherwise, plan your shelves to be only so wide as to hold the equipment intended and paint them with a glossy paint which can be easily wiped off with a damp cloth—preferably a standard darkroom paint, which resists chemical action, like Eastman's *Kodacoat.*

Whether you work in improvised darkroom or ideal laboratory, you need to equip it with essential working apparatus, which includes:

Darkroom Apron

The need to protect clothing is self-evident.

Safelight Lamp

The photographer must work in a *dark* room. But he needs to see to control results. With experience, he performs many operations in total darkness, such as developing panchromatic film. However, for developing orthochromatic film and for printing, safelight illumination aids the operator until he is thoroughly familiar with technic. The Eastman Brownie darkroom or safelight lamp, price $2, is suitable if you work in a small space. Other models are priced somewhat higher. Remember to use the safelight recommended for the film and paper you are working with. Series 2, with a 10-watt bulb, is correct for orthochromatic film. Series 0A takes care of most printing.

Trays

Size depends on the size of film you use. If 5 x 7, you will need two trays 8 x 10 and two 11 x 14, unless you are buying at the same time with an eye to making enlargements. However, the cost of using greater quantities of developer and hypo than you need in developing films and making contact prints should be weighed against the cost of buying two sets of trays. Enameled steel is recommended, though hard rubber or glass trays may also be used. The new stainless steel trays are good but expensive. Trays of other materials should not be used. As regards tanks, these are discussed in Chapter 7, with a recommendation.

Graduates

These should be preferably of glass, for cleanliness in measuring and mixing solutions, though there is danger of breakage. One 16-ounce and one 32-ounce graduate facilitate preparation of solutions.

Stirring Rod

Preferably of hard rubber, as the glass rods break easily.

Scale

You need a scale if you wish to make your own formulas. The standard studio type is suitable.

Interval Timer

For tray development, exact measurement of time is facilitated by a device which rings a bell at the end of the correct period. Use of a timer is especially important when you develop films in total darkness, as with panchromatic material. It is not essential to have a timer of the type used for printing, as printing time can be counted with the aid of any clock which has a second hand.

Thermometer

Measurement of temperature (in checking temperature of film developer and printing developer) is as important as measurement of time. The thermometer should read at least as high as 140 degrees, as chemicals usually have to be mixed at 125 degrees.

Towels

Cleanliness is indispensable to photography. Early learn the habit of washing hands after you have had them in the hypo. Otherwise you will contaminate the developing solutions, as well as mar film and paper.

Filter Cotton

To wipe off films when they are hung up to dry, which will decrease the danger of watermarks, etc. It is also used in photography for many other purposes, as in retouching, polishing prints, filtering solutions, etc.

Clips

A good, inexpensive type is made of wood. When hanging up films or prints, do not clip too far down on the negative or positive surface, or you will mar the picture area. If you hang up prints to dry, place clips at bottom to prevent curling.

Neg-a-Chart

The Neg-a-Chart is a guide to the kinds of negatives—"dense," "thin," "contrasty," "flat." The "average" or "normal" negative is marked "2" on the chart.

Negative Preservers

Glassine or cellophane envelopes are to be preferred. Since the film can be seen through its transparent covering, it does not have to be removed from the envelope so often, which obviates excessive handling with danger of fingermarks or scratches.

Printing Frame or Printer

Size depends on you, again. Arguments for the more expensive printer are stated in Chapter 8. The Agfa 5 x 7 printer costs $19.50. Printing frames of the same size cost about one-sixth as much. However, dodging can only be done practically with a printer.

Printing Lamp

If you choose the cheaper printing frame, you may use as a light source any desk lamp, floor lamp, drop light, or wall bracket within working distance of your table. Use a 75-watt bulb.

18. TRESTLE BRIDGE — MATTHEW BRADY

Primitiveness of the bridge echoes primitiveness of materials (wet plate and all) with which Brady had to make his masterly Civil War reportage.

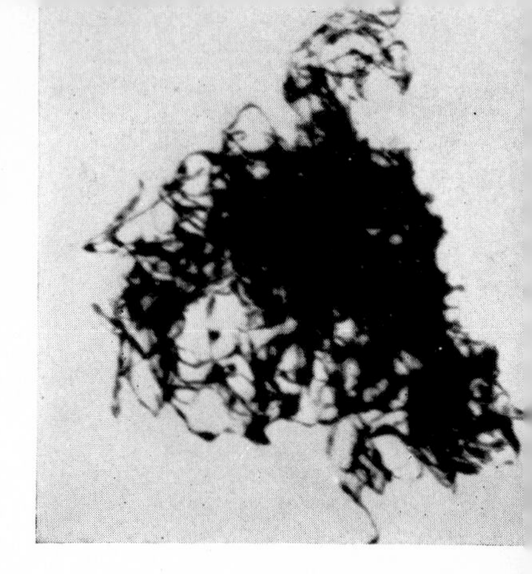

19.*a* WHAT AN EXPOSED FILM LOOKS LIKE

Photographs made on an electronic microscope constructed in the Eastman Research Laboratories show how a silver halide crystal which was exposed to light looks when developed in (left) hydroquinone and (right) amidol. The crystal is enlarged 40,000 times.

Courtesy of Eastman Kodak Company

19*b*. ELECTRONICS — BERENICE ABBOTT

Electronic Research.

Courtesy of Life Magazine and RCA Research Laboratories

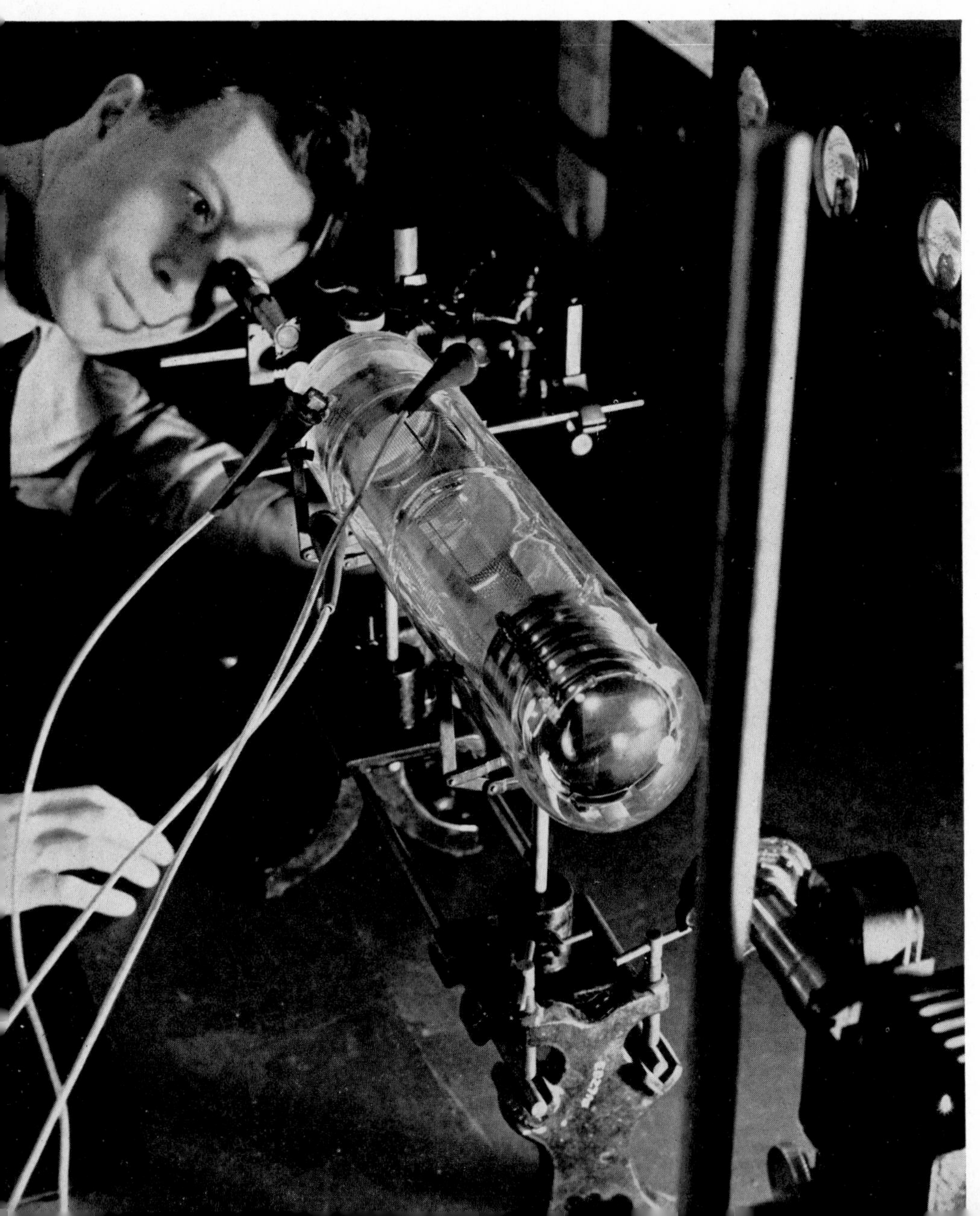

Bottles

For storing stock solutions, etc., use brown photographic bottles in quart or pint sizes. Label these with gummed stickers.

Syphon

For washing prints, a syphon is optional, though desirable.

Filter

If your water supply shows traces of rust or of foreign chemical substances like the alkalis, a filter attached to the faucet is an excellent accessory. The Elkay Photo-Pure Water Filter, price $3.15, is good for this purpose except that the filter pads have to be renewed frequently.

These items constitute the main fixed equipment you need, not including an enlarger. Then there is the question of supplies, which are used up from time to time, such as chemicals, film and paper. As far as chemicals are concerned, you will either supply yourself with the prepared formulas recommended for film developer, as Agfa 17 or Eastman D76, and the various formulas recommended for paper, which is a simple proposition, or you will indulge a secret taste of chemistry in compounding your solutions after all the tried and tested formulas. Morgan & Lester's *Photo-Lab-Index* is a useful reference work for laboratory enthusiasts. *Basic Photography* may be studied for the theory of photographic chemistry.

You need, in addition to the above, acid fixing powder (hypo) both for film and paper. Stock a small amount of potassium bromide to add to your developer for printing, as suggested in Chapter 9. You make a saturated solution by stirring the dry chemical into an ounce of water (preferably distilled) until the water will dissolve no more of the salt. Also stock acetic acid, 28 per cent, for the "acid short stop bath" in printing.

For general use, you will do well to stick to orthochromatic film, because it can be developed under a safelight, whereas panchromatic film has to be developed in complete darkness. Since orthochromatic film is cheaper, it is just as well to work with it until your grasp of photography requires the use of the more subtle and complicated panchromatic.

As for paper, normal contrast paper such as Azo No. 2 is adequate at first, developed with D72. Since we are trying to develop good habits of photographic practice, there is an advantage in confining ourselves to one grade of paper at this point, because this gives a constant factor in the extremely variable equation of exposure, developing and printing. The expert photographer naturally makes use of the latitude offered him by grades of paper to compensate for characteristics in negatives which he could not completely control. However, it is better to work toward better negatives, that is, negatives which will produce good prints on normal contrast papers. Later, the range of papers may be used when the best negative possible under given conditions has been made and it still needs compensation or adjustment.

If you already have an enlarger and have been working with it, you will naturally have a stock of projection paper on hand. But that is another story. Chapter 12 discusses grades and types of paper more fully.

7. Developing the Negative

WHEN Matthew Brady made his photographs of the American Civil War, he had only primitive instruments with which to work. Using the wet plate collodion process, he had to cover blank glass plate with sensitizing solution, put it in the camera, take his picture and develop the plate—all within ten minutes, and without accidentally exposing the plate. Despite tremendous physical handicaps, he created masterpieces. Today, photographic machines, materials and methods represent a great technical advance over Brady's time. Yet we too need to show as great concern for the minutiae of the photographic process as he did amid the battlefield's dangers and hazards. Our care is manifested in cleanliness, precision, attention to scientific detail. This is photography's equivalent for the craftsmanship shown by old-time artists who laboriously ground colors by hand.

Because industry has made great strides in the manufacture of fast film, it is more than ever necessary to remember that photography is an art based on exact measurements, where the laboratory's fine-gauged technic is needed. In Brady's time, primitiveness of machine and materials did not prevent him from creating authentic works of art. It did, however, mean that the tempo of his photographs was vastly slower than the tempo of our age when split seconds are equal to the minutes and even hours of nineteenth century exposures. Just because we are able to work with miniature cameras, fast film, fine-grain developers, we have to observe even greater care in handling these delicate objects and materials.

Not only must we expose and develop prints exactly the right length of time. We must measure light, time and similar factors with mathematical conscientiousness in order that our negatives shall be correctly exposed. After that, development is an equally meticulous step in the photographic sequence. My plea to learn photography correctly applies particularly to developing. Guard against the temptation to false economy. Do not use stale developer; it is cheaper to buy chemicals than to waste film and your time. Do not experiment blindly with directions on prepared developer, nor, when you work with more elaborate formulas, with their proportions. Be careful not to scratch the film when handling it in the developer and hypo. Carelessness is fatal at any step but especially so in developing film; for mistakes made at this point cannot be corrected.

What Is a Negative?

The answer is simple. It is film which has been exposed to light and then developed so that the lights and darks make a picture, but in reverse. Printing from the negative gives the positive print or photograph. But since photography did not spring into being full grown, to arrive at the negative and positive required years of effort. Today flexible film, whether roll film, cut film or film pack, which is so easily handled by millions of photographers, represents the climax of those early experiments. Indeed, not till photography evolved the flexible film base in 1888 could it achieve the stature of a universal art.

The effect of this invention Taft has discussed in his excellent *Photography and the American Scene*. First of all, it made possible the folding camera for amateurs. He writes (pp. 388-9): "The camera was small, 6¾ inches long by 3¾ inches deep and wide, weighed twenty-two ounces, and made a picture 2½ inches in diameter. Loaded with a spool of film of sufficient length for one hundred exposures, the camera sold for twenty-five dollars. It was reloaded (in the dark) by the dealer for ten dollars; the exposed roll was developed by the dealer or sent to Rochester to be processed. It may be said in passing that the introduction of this camera marked the beginning of an extensive new business, that of the photo-finisher." The human and esthetic significance of the new invention were triumphantly prophesied in the *Scientific American* of September 15, 1888 (Taft: Note 407): "We predict for it a very general use—it promises to make the practice of photography well nigh universal."

Yet universal as photography is today and indispensable as flexible film is, film itself is practically an unknown quantity. What we are accustomed to seeing and handling with nonchalant ease is the exposed and developed film, the negative. Film because of its light-sensitive character is better known by its packaging than by itself.

Photographic film consists of a base (glass plate or transparent celluloid base) coated with a gelatin emulsion holding in colloidal suspension grains of silver bromide. It is manufactured in darkness, with all precautions to standardize gelatin, silver content and thickness of emulsion. Film is exposed by allowing light to reach it through the lens opening in the camera, a "latent image" then being produced by the photochemical action of light striking on silver salts imbedded in the light-sensitive emulsion. By latent image, we mean an image not visible to the eye but capable of being developed by a suitable chemical solution. To convert latent image into visible image, we develop the film.

This brief description is made to underline the necessity for great care in all manual operations connected with the handling of film, whether in development, printing, retouching, filing or visual examination. Manufacturers of photographic materials use elaborate and costly sensitometers to control the character and quality of film. Photographers should show equal respect by manipulating their delicate materials carefully and with good technic.

There is no mystery about developing a film. As the result of exposure (through the lens of the camera) the silver salts in the emulsion have undergone a chemical change. Development consists of treating the exposed film —in darkness—with a solution (called developer) to reduce the exposed salts to metallic silver. Then, after rinsing, the film is placed in another solution (called acid fixing bath) to remove the unexposed salts. After fixing, the film is washed thoroughly and dried; and we have the negative, in which the parts affected by light are dark and parts less affected are lighter, a reversal of the relation of light and dark in the photographed object.

You need in developing, besides a darkroom in which to work, developer, fixing bath, water and containers for solutions. Suitable developers and acid fixing bath (hypo) may be purchased in any supply store. The packages give simple instructions for preparing proper solutions. Follow these instructions and remember that cleanliness is a primary rule.

There are two methods of developing, by tray and by tank. For roll film, tank is more sensible and, indeed, 35 mm. film can only be developed by tank. (See Consumers Union Reports, August, 1940, pp. 9-11, for data on tanks.) For cut film or film pack, I prefer tray development unless there is a large number of films to be developed. If you have followed my recommendation and are working with a fair sized ground glass camera, you may as well cut the cost of equipment for the time being and stick to tray development. I write this consideredly. There is a tendency in photography to believe that all your problems will be solved if you have quantities of equipment. Experience teaches that success is achieved by simplifying both equipment and procedure. This even leads me to say some thing as radical as "Don't use tanks."

When you develop by tray, one rule is of prime importance: constantly move and rock the tray to agitate the developer so that it is always in contact with all parts of the film. For tray development, you have supplied yourself with four trays as specified in Chapter 6. The usual practice is for righthanded people to work from left to right—developer at the left, rinse bath in the middle, and hypo at the right. However, to fill the trays, the order is from right to left: first fill the hypo tray, then the water rinse bath, and finally the developer tray. This order is necessary to prevent hypo from splashing into the developer.

When developing film packs, remember that they require one-third more time than cut film. The procedure is the same, except that the protective paper must be torn off before the films are placed in the developer. There is certainly a practical argument against developing film packs in tanks because they have to be removed from the tank and placed in the hypo in a tray, so that there is no great economy of labor and the films themselves are subjected to extra handling with the consequent extra risk of being scratched or marred.

A few more points on good technic. Mix chemicals into water, not vice versa. Be sure to wash your thermometer thoroughly after you have tested the temperature of the hypo, before using it in the developer. Or better still, if you are careful not to "swap" them, use one thermometer for hypo, and a second one for developer. Be careful not to splash hypo, as its dry particles make spots on negatives and prints.

In developing, you are profiting by the one controlled method in photography—time and temperature development. As said previously, other steps of the photograph process have not yet reached the stage of complete scientific control. But in development, you have no alibi. Make the solution correctly, use it at the temperature and for the time (minimum) given, following instructions to agitate the film in the developer. Then, whatever errors crop up, the fault is yours. Here experience can be of great value; for by studying failures, you make possible your future successes. Therefore, keep the developer at the prescribed 65 degrees Fahrenheit. If necessary, place the tray containing developer in a larger tray of cold water, using ice as a last resort. If you are one of those handy souls who love nothing better than hammer and saw, you can easily find blueprints for building a waterbath.

Whether you use tray or tank, the temperature of the developer at the beginning of development should be 65 degrees. A slight spread from 62 to 68 degrees may be permitted, but with proportionate changes in the length of development time. But over 70 degrees, development is errative because it is too fast. As a result, negatives are too dense, the gelatin emulsion swells and produces coarse grain and is also more easily scratched. Too rapid development causes unevenness and exhausts the developer quickly. On the other hand, developing at temperatures noticeably lower than 65 degrees is also to be avoided. For the hydroquinone in the solution ceases to act and shadow detail is lost, producing a too contrasty negative. At lower temperatures, longer development is required, which aside from technical and esthetic results is to be avoided because it wastes time and labor. For conditions where it is impossible to control temperature, developers like Panthermic 777 permit the photographer to break the above rules. On the whole, however, sticking to the rules is the best way to master photography. Indeed, the sign of the master is that he knows when and why he is breaking the rules; the novice breaks them without knowing—and without being able to control the result.

Cut film is slid into the developer and kept constantly in motion, so that the separate negatives will not stick to each other. The tray should be rocked frequently during development. For general work, a moderately fine-grain developer, such as Agfa 17 or Eastman D76, is to be preferred. There is no objection to the use of very fine-grain developers for larger size film, as well as 35 mm., unless you plan to do retouching on the negative.

After the rinse bath, the film must be moved about in the hypo for at least two or three minutes. Then it is left to fix for fifteen minutes, with occasional agitation. Finally, it should be washed for twenty minutes, in gently running water, or with occasional changes of water. In working back and forth from hypo to developer, be sure always to wash your hands after they have been in the hypo and before putting them again in the developer.

Before you hang up the films to dry, wipe the surface free from scum or sediment with wet cotton under water, care being taken not to scratch or mar the softened emulsion. Cut film is hung up by the corner. Excess moisture should be wiped off with clean cotton wrung out in water.

All these admonitions may sound monotonously routine. But they are essential in the campaign for good, clean photographic technic.

8. Printing the Negative

PHOTOGRAPHS are prints made from negatives, reconverting the values of light and shade to the original state. Without good prints, photography cannot hope to realize its potentialities for art, communication, recreation, science and commerce. Misconceptions as to photography's artistic value explain why many photographers do not learn how to print well. Yet if a photographer cannot control his work to its final visual expression, can he be said really to be "making" his picture?

The amateur never really learns what is wrong with his negatives if he leaves their printing to the corner drugstore photofinisher. But if he has some knowledge of printing, he can judge better what results to expect from a negative and how to distinguish a negative's faults. Mastering printing confers other benefits. The scale of nature is so vast that when a new photographer goes out to take a picture, he cannot encompass the entire scene. But in his small print, nature is reduced to a scale more easily comprehended by his eye, which thus receives valuable training for more difficult subjects. In the developer, the photographer's creative vision comes alive; but not until the print is made, does he achieve a completed statement of the reality he imagined when he clicked the shutter. To fail to master printing is to miss half the fun of photography.

We begin printing by making a contact print. Later we'll take up projection printing for enlargements and the intricate subject of the art of printing.

What Is a Good Print?

A good print is clear, rich, luminous. It suggests the relations of nature's colors by tones ranging from purest white to deepest black. Even the untrained eye can distinguish rich blacks and whites and washed out neutral grays. In printing, always try to reproduce the tonal relations of the original subject. Black and white are as much colors as the primary red, blue and yellow. Only, their quality is more reticent and aloof; its charm grows with long association. In fact, you will find the excellent photographer Paul Strand consciously working to achieve "warm" and "cold" tones in his prints, according to the character of the subject. This may be done by gold toning, manipulation of developers, platinum paper, etc.

Luminosity is perhaps the most beautiful single characteristic of the photographic print, which makes the beholder feel that the picture is flooded with light—as indeed the subject itself was to be taken. A good photograph suggests sunlight even on photographic paper. Here is a test by which you may judge the success of your work.

As with developing, good technic is essential. The first precaution in printing (which must become the photographer's second nature) is to take due care for the sensitive character of printing paper. Photographic paper has one side (the sensitive side) coated with gelatin in which silver salts are evenly imbedded. This emulsion turns black when exposed to white light and must, therefore, be handled in a darkroom, shielded from light. Series OA safelight, yellowish-green in color, is used for contact printing. If white light falls directly on the paper, it will be "light-struck." If light leaks into the darkroom or if the safelight is not really "safe," the paper may be "fogged," a common fault with amateurs' prints. Hence the necessity for underlining this warning.

As in developing film, lay out your trays and prepare them, left to right—developer, acid rinse water and hypo, remembering that the trays should always be clean and they should be filled from right to left, so that hypo will not splash into the developer. Printing frame or printer is ready, as well as a proper light source. You have a stock of paper on hand, preferably a contact paper of normal contrast like Eastman Azo No. 2. Glossy single weight is suitable. Use with this paper Eastman D72 developer. And now let's print.

What Is Printing?

In printing, you apply chemical principles similar to those made use of in developing the negative. The paper (on which the final "print" or

20. A NEWHAVEN SAILOR — David Octavius Hill

Printed by Hill and Adamson from a paper negative made between 1843 and 1848.

Metropolitan Museum of Art

21. JOE GOULD — BERENICE ABBOTT

Taken with 5 x 7 view camera; studio lighting.

photograph is made) is coated with an emulsion containing silver salts. In the dark room, you direct white light through the negative onto the paper. The exposed paper is developed, rinsed, fixed, washed and dried, much as the negative was. You now have a positive image, like the original subject in the relation of its lights and darks. The first photographs (daguerreotypes) were reversed in value because the principle of the negative had not yet been discovered and these "sun pictures" were made directly on light-sensitive silvered metal plates. Besides being unique copies, the daguerreotypes are difficult to see because of their chemical composition, although very beautiful in the shimmering, delicate tonalities of their reversed images. Not till Fox Talbot discovered the paper negative through his experiments with the calotype was it possible for photographers to make more than one picture from one exposure. The negative enormously widened photography's physical range and gave photography its popular character as a multiple original medium. More than that, it made possible various improvements and extensions of technical and esthetic scope, such as retouching, enlarging, cropping, etc., which have now been assimilated into the legitimate photographic idiom.

Printing is almost the last step in getting the photograph before the world—whether the world of the millions of readers of a magazine like *Life* or the intimate world of your home circle. Printing takes that reverse image of the negative—in which blacks of the original are light and whites are dark—and turns them back to their natural tones. The positive image obtained by printing is capable of indefinite multiplication by a phenomenon which is simple yet miraculous. Again, light is the agent. Light-sensitive paper is placed in direct contact with the negative, emulsion to emulsion, either in printing frame or in printer, and light is directed through the transparent film onto the paper. A second latent image has been created, to be made visible in the developing solution.

If there is any question as to which is the sensitive side of the negative, remember that it looks *dull.* If you place the wrong side of the negative to the paper's sensitive side, you will get a "mirror" image. This may be all right, unless there is text to be read on signs or people shaking hands with their left hands. The sensitive side of printing paper may be distinguished by the fact that it curves inward slightly. Look at the paper under the safelight and note differences in texture between sensitive side and paper base.

The latter, having no coating, will show a fiber-like surface. If in doubt, bite a corner of the paper. The sensitive side sticks to the teeth.

In printing, as in developing, the first standard to enforce is that of time and temperature. If the temperature of the developing solution is kept at 70 degrees, then uniform prints may be obtained by ascertaining correct length of time for exposure and developing all prints for the same length of time, which is 45 seconds. This involves simple procedures. The trays have already been set out and filled, the working sequence being (as in developing film) from left to right and the order of filling from right to left. The only difference is that the rinse bath has had 1½ ounces of 28 per cent acetic acid added to 32 ounces of water as an "acid short stop bath."

In printing, the darkroom operator exposes the paper, either in a printing frame or printer, allowing white light (such as ordinary electric light) to pass through the negative. The transparent parts of the negative allow light to pass through according to the degree of transparency, and the dense parts prevent light from reaching the paper with as great intensity as through the transparent. When the exposed paper is developed, the latent positive image emerges as a visible picture.

As with all processing, the first step is to turn off all the bright lights and turn on the safelight. For printing with all papers, except fast bromide papers for enlarging, the Series OA safelight is correct. Open your package of paper, and tear a sheet into a number of test strips, to make trials for proper exposure. Carefully shield the paper from any white light. Before you start printing, be sure the glass in printing frame or printer is perfectly clean. If necessary, wash it with soap and water on both sides and see that no fingermarks or dust streaks are left to ornament the final print. Brush the frame or printer to remove loose dust. In placing negative and paper in frame or printer, do not touch the surface of either film or paper. Learn to handle both by their edges. Place the negative in the printing frame with the emulsion (dull) side away from the glass. The film (shiny) side should be in contact with the glass. The procedure is slightly different in detail if you use a printer, though the principle is the same. In that case, follow instructions which come with the machine.

Now place your test strip face down on the negative, selecting the center of interest of your picture to test. Cover paper and film with the printing frame back, and lock. Place the frame flat on the table, face up, with light source so adjusted that it is at the correct distance. This distance is twice the diagonal of the frame, so that roughly the distance would be for a 4 x 5 frame one foot, for a 5 x 7 one and a half feet, and for an 8 x 10 two feet. Now make your exposure test. In this connection, exposure means the length of time the sensitive paper, covered by the negative, is exposed to white light. So snap on the printing lamp for ten seconds only, either counting the seconds or watching the second hand of your timepiece. Snap off the printing light, and write "10 sec." on the back of the strip.

Place the test strip, emulsion side up, in the developer, sliding it beneath the surface so that it is quickly and evenly covered. Gently rock the tray to break air bubbles and to insure even development over the entire surface. Develop exactly 45 seconds. Then remove to the acid rinse bath. After rinsing a few seconds, quickly transfer strip to the hypo. It should go into the hypo face up and immediately be submerged and moved about, then turned face down. The fixing bath stops the action of the developer and "fixes" the images. After 15 seconds in the hypo, the test strip may be examined under white light. Remember that after you have had your hands in the hypo, they must be washed before you put them in the developer again.

Correct exposure is imperative. Hence the reason for making test strips. Exposure depends on: (1) density of negative; (2) strength of light; (3) distance of the printing frame from the light; and (4) length of time exposed. To simplify calculations, always use the same strength of light. In contact printing, correct exposure is attained when the print develops slowly but fully in 45 seconds with the developer at 70 degrees Fahrenheit and the paper of normal contrast.

Before making a print, repeat the test several times, varying the time of exposure slightly, until you get a "normal" image, that is, one which seems natural to you in relation to your recollection of the original subject. Mark on each strip length of exposure. Develop each, rinse and fix, so that they may be studied more carefully. Be careful each time you take a piece of paper from the envelope to protect the package of printing paper from all light except the safelight. If your first test strip is very pale or blank, your negative is too dense. Try doubling or tripling the time of exposure. If the image on your first test strip appeared in the developer too rapidly or gave too dark an image, the paper was overexposed. For further tests, reduce the exposure time.

Having made a test strip with approximately correct exposure, you may—if you wish to experiment—make full-sized prints of ten different exposures, ranging say from one to ten seconds. Be sure to mark length of exposure on the back of each print before placing it in the developer. Develop, rinse, fix, turn on the light and compare prints. It may be that the time of exposure for the center of interest is correctly gauged but does not apply to all parts of the negative. This leads to the question of dodging, which will be discussed in the chapters on "Enlarging" and "The Art of Printing." It is difficult to do much of this legitimate kind of print control with the printing frame.

When handling prints in the hypo, do not splash. Handle them gently in all solutions without splashing chemicals, but especially in the hypo. Hypo is a bad enemy because it crystallizes when dry and floats about the darkroom, making spots on negatives, prints and clothes. Prints should not remain in the hypo more than 15 or less than 12 minutes. They should be thoroughly fixed; and since they do not fix themselves by lying passively in the acid fixing bath, they should be frequently agitated, turned and separated. Thorough agitation is especially important when the print is first put into the hypo.

After fixing, the next step is to wash the prints, in order to wash the hypo completely out of the paper's emulsion and fiber. Washing is as important as developing and fixing. It must be done thoroughly if the print is not to turn yellow and fade. Double weight paper needs to be washed longer than single weight. Washing may be done in several ways. One way is to change the water in the tray twelve times at 5-minute intervals. Another way is to run water into and out of the tray for at least an hour, provided that the prints are separated and turned frequently and that the stream of running water is not directed at their surface. Moving, turning, separating, are indispensable to eliminate the hypo. A tray syphon is excellent for this purpose.

Prints are hung up to dry by clips, which are also used as weights on the bottom. Wipe off the prints with clean cotton wrung out in water, to remove excess moisture.

22. JOHN WATTS — BERENICE ABBOTT
Taken with 8 x 10 Century Universal view camera; 1 second; f/32.
Applies principles of lenses and swings.

23. CABRIOLET — Eugène Atget

Taken with 18 x 24 cm. view camera; rapid rectilinear lens; glass plate. For composition, see Chapter 15.

Collection of Berenice Abbott

9. Analyzing the Photograph

NOW that you've developed the film and printed it, are you satisfied? There are many reasons why you may not be. Does the photograph express what you saw when you took the picture? Elementary yet essential steps are laid down here for analysis to enable you to make the most of your photographs. But before going into more complicated diagnoses, there is a simple precaution to take. Is the print "fogged?" Does a gray veil seem to cover the print, and is the sensation of light absent? Are the whites gray, and the values flat?

"Fogging" is caused by light leaking into the darkroom from outside or by an unsafe darkroom lamp. To test your darkroom's lighttightness, place an unexposed test strip under the safelight and cover part of it with a coin. Leave for four minutes, then develop and fix. If you can see the shape of the coin as white and the rest of the paper as gray, white light is coming into the darkroom from some source. Turn off the the safelight, and repeat the experiment in darkness. If your test strip still shows fogging, light is leaking into the darkroom from outside. If the strip is white, then the safelight is leaking light and you will have to patch it up as best you can, or buy a new one.

Having eliminated this relatively minor trouble. Let's look at your prints. A common fault in printing is to take the prints from the developer too soon. If you do so, because the wet paper looks deceptively dark under the dim safelight, you will be disappointed; under bright white light, the prints will appear crude and unfinished. Washed and dried, they are unsatisfactory. Contact prints developed the full 45 seconds have quality and tonal unity. Look at the print during development and seek to see it as a whole and note if it has "roundness" and three-dimensional effect.

Assume that you have developed the print the correct length of time.

Does it still fail to satisfy you, and you can't decide why? Perhaps the high lights lack detail. Remedy: expose for detail in the high lights. Now are the shadows too black? If so, then the negative was either overdeveloped or underexposed, or both, with the result that contrast between high lights and shadows is too great in the print. Shadow detail in the film will not register in the print unless the negative is properly balanced. If the negative lacks balance, shadows must be dodged, or otherwise held back, to produce satisfactory high lights in the print. The problem is to learn how to make negatives with a correct exposure-development relation for normal paper.

Are the edges of your print pale and chalky? One of the commonest headaches of photography is "edge intensification." This means that the edges are denser than the rest of the negative. Such areas must be given additional light during printing by dodging, which can only be done conveniently in contact printing with a printer.

More about high lights. Do they look gray or lack zip? Very often, especially with softer grades of paper, two or three additional drops of potassium bromide (saturated solution) in the developer will keep the whites whiter and brighten the print's whole appearance. Do the high lights of your prints look "grainy?" Then, even with longer printing exposure, you will not get detail; for the high light areas of the negative are too dense to print right, due to overdevelopment of the film. Moral: develop less the next time.

The above suggests that no one step of the photographic process is separable from the other steps. At every point, we come up against the question of what kind of negative you are working with. This involves two kinds of criticism, creative and technical. First of all, place your negative on a sheet of clean white paper face down. Study it in terms of reversed tones, that is, imagining the dark areas as light and the light areas as dark, as the print will appear. Form the habit of studying your negatives for possible faults.

Perhaps the negative was fogged? The test is simple. Are the borders clear and transparent? If they are gray instead, the negative was fogged. And you know what to do about it. Are any areas of the film (exclusive of the borders) entirely transparent? If so, the film was underexposed or the lighting was unbalanced. There should be no completely transparent areas in a negative; for during the time light strikes the silver salts when the camera shutter is clicked, whether it be for 1/10, 1/25, or 1/50 of a second, enough light should have reached the light-sensitive emulsion to have affected some silver particles all over the film.

A good negative should have ample shadow detail. But at the same time, it should be fairly "thin," otherwise excessively dense parts will affect the print's high lights as described above. High lights in prints from over-developed negatives lack detail and form. In the negative this fault shows up as high light areas which are too dense and "blocked up." If shadow detail is present in the negative and high lights are too dark, the film is over-developed. This makes for too much contrast and results in flat high lights in the print. Furthermore the negative requires long printing exposure because it is dense. By "reading" the negative, you can tell whether the film has been adequately exposed. From your best final print, you can tell whether the film was properly developed. By carrying out the experiment outlined in Chapter 17, you can determine a working method for exposure-development balance.

Negatives may be dense, flat, contrasty, thin, dense and flat, or thin and flat. In fact, they may have any number of several characteristics, or a combination. The principle I advise is: *expose for shadows and develop for high lights.* There are several schools of thought on this subject, however, and a personal style is evolved with experience. Your style has to do with your philosophical approach to photography. If you are a realist, photography means accurate rendering of materials and surfaces, documentary precision, clean cut definition, all possible sharpness, texture, detail. For you, then, shadow detail will be a must. To achieve this, so that your photographs may be as expressive as possible, you need to work for adequate exposure. Having seen thousands of students' negatives, I am convinced that fully nine-tenths of them are underexposed. On this point, I am heartily in agreement with P. H. Emerson, who wrote in *Naturalistic Photography* in 1889: "Underexposure gives chalky whites and sooty blacks, *ergo,* no tonality, *ergo,* worthless. No remedy, destroy at once."

The tendency to overdevelop film is all too common. It is probable that developing time, as stated on most manufacturers' instructions, is too long. It may be that this is deliberate, to compensate for the photographer's tendency to underexpose the negative. If so, it is a bad remedy for a bad disease. For better results, use the minimum developing time given as your maximum. These procedures are always relative, however, and must be gradually evolved. A time suitable for one person is not necessarily satisfactory for another because of the varying factors of type of lens, shutter, film, enlarger, etc. But if you keep in the back of your head the fact that you are aiming for a negative the exposure and development of which will be of a character to print best on *normal* paper, many of your headaches will disappear.

Besides these rather complicated problems of exposure and development of negative and print, there are minor points of correct technical procedure, which can make or mar your work. The necessity for keeping films free from fingermarks and free from contamination from soiled tables or shelves is not fully realized. You may obtain a negative which is perfectly exposed and developed and a print from it, also perfectly exposed and developed, but the final result ruined by defects due to lack of cleanliness.

The importance of good laboratory procedure may be gauged by the ravages of incorrect technic. Streaks appear on the film's surface if the developer has not acted evenly on the entire surface. Hence, the exhortation to agitate the film frequently in the developer. Uneven fixing also produces streaked films because if certain areas continue to develop in the hypo, they become darker than those areas in which developing has been stopped by the acid fixing bath's neutralizing action. Milky areas are due to insufficient fixing, because all the undeveloped silver salts have not been dissolved out of the film's emulsion. Watermarks are due to incorrect wiping and drying. Another fault, though not easily detected in a newly developed negative, results from insufficient washing. If hypo remains on the film, it will turn yellow in the course of time. Ditto for prints.

After all this, you would think that your problems were all solved. Not at all. Now you face some esthetic aspects of photography. Your exposure may have been perfect. You may have developed the negative correctly and printed it admirably. And yet still you are not happy. The picture does not look the way you imagined it would. Why?

Could it be composition? Instinct plays an invaluable part in picture-making. If you were to take a photograph blindly without any planning or selection, you would be startled to see how unhappy, unbalanced and uninteresting the result. The importance of consciously composing your picture so that it has balance and unity cannot be overestimated. That story, however, is taken up in Chapter 15. But even the newest photographer, fresh out in the world with his box camera, instinctively seeks to make his picture a complete pictorial entity. Lack of experience, of course, accounts for his failures.

The mistakes made by newcomers to photography—and even by old hands—follow well defined patterns. Most frequent, perhaps, is the tendency to take the picture with its center of interest too far away. Possibly you saw a handsome subject from across the street or several blocks away. In the photograph, the subject which enticed you is dwarfed; instead of being imposing and majestic (as it seemed to your inner eye) it is revealed as small and insignificant. Don't be afraid of your subject; approach it boldly. Get as big an image as possible consistent with your lens' capacity and your own understanding of the subject's pictorial character. Arrange the picture on the ground glass so as to eliminate extraneous and unnecessary objects, so that the subject which first captured your imagination and appeared to you in so commanding a light will be recreated in a similar mood in your photograph.

Another mistake frequently made is that the camera is not carefully aimed. Result: feet, ears, top of head, all cut off with the casual abandon of the Red Queen's "Off with his head!" If you are photographing a child, don't get too near—photography is paradoxical, you will think; but for the moment just forget the last paragraph—unless you can also manage to keep the camera low, in the plane of the child's height.

A don't about foregrounds. Unless they contribute to the picture's meaning, there is no reason for having big, empty five-acre lots filling up two-thirds of the space. When taking your picture, see that its area is not divided in the middle either vertically or horizontally. It may merely be a question of choosing your point of view more carefully and of relating your subject more interestingly to its background.

Height of camera is a further consideration. Often it should be placed higher than floor or street level. A chair, door step, roof, window, fire escape, may offer a better height from which to organize your composition.

Finally, perspective offers one of the most interesting problems of picture-making. By withdrawing from or approaching your subject more closely, you have a choice of perspectives—either more natural or more distorted, according to the effect you wish to create. In some cases, the more pronounced or acute your perspective the more interesting the picture, and the more difficult it is to take. Then you need "swings" (see Chapter 11) or perhaps you can do the trick by closing down the lens. My photograph of John Watts (Pl. 22) illustrates how an exaggerated perspective creates the psychological reality of the subject. The many thousands who hurry by Trinity Churchyard daily see the statue and the Irving Trust Building facade in a hasty impressionistic visual distortion. From the optical point of view, it was necessary to distort in order to encompass both statue and facade in one shot. The photograph has telescoped or condensed space into its dimensions; there is a kind of urgency or haste in the visual presentation, as there is in the subject in real life.

Related to composition is lighting. What light effect do you want in your picture? Is the lighting flat and uninteresting? The intuitive photographer often passes up an otherwise interesting subject because the light does not bring out the subject to best advantage. So if you take photography seriously, study the way light falls naturally on various subjects. It is helpful to watch familiar scenes at different times of day (just as Monet painted the Rouen cathedral at different hours and in different seasons) and to observe how the change of angle and quality of light dramatizes a subject. Better still, photograph the same subject under different lighting conditions and see what happens.

Shadows enhance composition. Usually a front flat light (that is, a light from the sun when it is high overhead and directly back of the photographer) does not help a picture, though there may be exceptions. Even walking to another point of view will show you how the subject looks under slightly different light. An example of the difference lighting makes is my story of photographing the New York Stock Exchange, told and illustrated in Chapter 4.

In other words, if you want your pictures to be interesting and beautiful, you have to spend time and thought on them. Take a few pictures carefully and thoughtfully rather than shoot dozens, as if you were reeling off footage on a movie camera.

To sum up, what are you looking for in your photographs? Esthetic considerations aside, what makes a "good" photograph?

1. A good photograph is sharp. The principal object of interest has been focused with the foreground and background in proper relation.

2. The exposure has been correctly timed. Essential shadow detail has been fully registered.

3. The length of development for the film has been estimated exactly. The time was not too short, resulting in thin, flat negatives; nor was it too long, resulting in too contrasty negatives.

4. Negatives are clean, because the chemicals used were pure and the solutions worked with were at the correct temperatures. Negatives have been developed to a low contrast with fine grain.

5. The print has been exposed and developed at the correct temperature in fresh developer; and it has been thoroughly fixed and washed.

These are *material* standards for good photography, on which the permanence of your work depends. Intangible but just as important standards will be discussed later.

10. Learning To See: The Lens

PHOTOGRAPHY is a new vision of life, a profoundly realistic and objective view of the external world. In the all-seeing and minute observation of the camera eye, we see what we never saw before—wealth of minutiae, broad panorama of earth and sky. What the human eye observes casually and incuriously, the eye of the camera (the lens) notes with relentless fidelity. Position of the sun, height of the tides, wrecked automobile captured in a "spot news" shot—these are facts which may or may not have esthetic significance. But they are *facts*, set forth by photography with convincing detail, facts sometimes so important in the objective sense that photographs are produced in law courts as infallible witnesses to truth.

This unique and powerful quality has established an esthetic based on realism as the new vision of life. But the photographic esthetic could not function without the tools which science has given photography. Very well for Eastman to bring forth the roll film in 1888; but if Petzval had not a half century earlier perfected a double lens for portraiture, photography would have had no impetus at its very birth to make progress and indeed might have languished and died away. In its hundred years of life, progress has been great, and in no field more than in the field of lenses. However, photographers still fail to bridge the chasm between the lens and the eye. They accept the lens as being identical with or equal to the eye. On this fallacy, many a fine picture is wrecked.

Because the human eye has great powers of accommodation, adjusting itself to wide angles of view, distortions of perspective and other aberrations of optical vision which the lens registers uncompromisingly, we are accustomed to see the external world in a fictitious not to say glamorous mood. Psychological memories and overtones color what our eyes think they see; our mental pictures are as much conventions of sight as the elaborate conventions of Rennaissance or Chinese art.

The camera eye is less easily imposed on. It demands logical and reasonable reality in what it records. It creates a marvelous record of fact, of truth, an almost microscopic chronicle of things, but according to its own character, a character mercilessly controlled by optics. What the lens sees is a single image at the instant the shutter is clicked. Unlike the human eye, the lens does not merge or superimpose images from what it saw a moment before or what it may see a moment after. It does not color the image it records with remembered images of other times and places. Nor does it include in its sharp, restricted, instantaneous view what is seen vaguely and indistinctly from the corner of the human eye. The lens freezes time and space in what may be an optical slavery or, contrarily, the crystallization of meaning. The limits of the lens' vision are esthetically often a virtue. However the limits create problems.

The spreading vistas of a city skyline, the towering heights of city skyscrapers, are obstacles it overcomes, but at a price. Distortion of parallel vertical lines, for example, is sometimes unavoidable to encompass the sweep of buildings a thousand feet high. Yet the human eye, accustomed to make an optical accommodation which the lens cannot, is estranged by distortion. Psychologically as well as physiologically, we see those vertical lines as parallel. When they appear disguised in the photograph, converging toward each other, we suffer a shock of unreality. The lens has contradicted its own nature of being the spokesman of reality. The real world, in which we rooted ourselves, has been destroyed. For reasons like this, to reconcile the lens' unswerving vision with human eye's flexible and imaginative vision is the task of all photographers not content with a blindly mechanical use of photography.

The first battle is won when you are able to translate what you see with your roving human eye into terms of what the lens will see. The second is to broaden the scope of the lens' optical vision, a not impossible though not too easy feat, as I shall explain in the next chapter on "Swings." The interesting essay in *U. S. Camera 1941,* Volume 2, by Dr. Alston Callahan on "The Camera and the Eye" provides a basis for understanding similarities and differences between human eye and camera eye. A technical reference is R. Kingslake's "How to Choose a Lens" in *Graphic Graflex Photography,* while *Basic Photography's* section on "Photographic Optics" gives an excellent analysis of the theory of lenses. To be a good photographer, you do not need to know the whole of optics. But in general, you will find it easier to solve problems of photographic expression if you understand lenses and how to use them.

You can make a photograph by letting light pass through a pinhole onto a film. But the exposure takes hours, because very little light is admitted, a tiny hole being required if the image is to be sharp. If we make the opening larger to let in more light and so to speed up exposure, we get a blurred image because of the flood of uncontrolled light.

The answer to photography's problem was the law of refraction, that is, the bending or refracting of rays of light. An elementary proposition of physics is that the direction of light rays is changed by passing them through a transparent medium, usually a glass prism. Light rays are bent when they enter the prism and when they leave it. We have all seen how an arm or stick appears bent when it is partly in and partly out of water. Such an optical image has been refracted.

Making use of refraction, the lens comes into the photographic picture. A lens acts, in effect as if two prisms had been put base to base, bending the rays of light toward each other so that they converge at a point. Used instead of a pinhole to admit light, the lens brings all the rays of light together in a much brighter image than is possible with the pinhole, while the principle of refraction makes it possible to obtain a sharp image. Length of exposure is decreased, and photographs can be made under practical working conditions. In the early days of photography, exposures hours long were made, due to the primitiveness not only of lenses but also of light-sensitive materials.

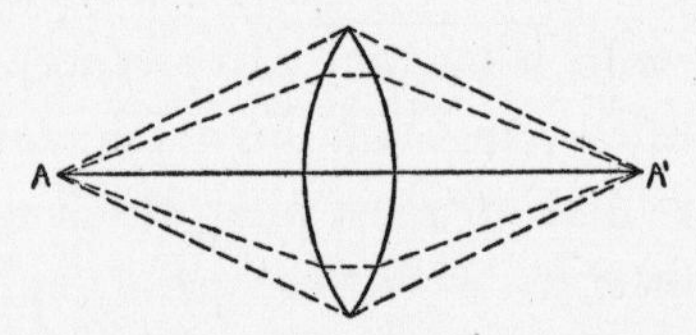

This diagram illustrates the principle. A is a point on the object photographed. Light rays travel from A in all directions and reach the lens where their direction is refracted and reversed and they meet again at A′, which is called the focal point. Thus we are able to use a great quantity of light rays emanating from A instead of the single thin beam that could enter through a pinhole. It is clear, however, that the film must be placed exactly at A′, the focal point where the converging light rays meet. The distance from the lens to the focal point is called the focal length.

A camera is generally supplied with a lens of focal length equal to the diagonal of the film used. A 4 x 5 inch view camera needs a 6 or 7 inch lens to insure adequate "covering power," that is, to make an evenly defined and illuminated image over the entire film.

Focal length determines the size of the image. The longer the focal length the larger the image; and conversely. Suppose we photograph a tree with a 3-inch lens, placing the camera at a distance to obtain an image one inch high. Now, without moving the camera, we use a 6-inch lens, that is, the lens must be six inches away from the film instead of three to be in focus. The second image will be two inches high instead of one inch. For the size of the image is proportional to the focal length of the lens. On the same size film, the longer focal length lens giving the larger image includes less of the subject, while the shorter focal length giving the smaller image includes more.

There is always a temptation to use too short a focal length lens, because it costs less and is smaller and lighter in weight. The risk is that to obtain a large image the photographer will get too close to his subject, with resulting fatal distortion of perspective. The most common example is the sort of snapshot in which a bather's feet (closest to the camera) are bigger than his entire torso. Furthermore, the perspective only obtainable with a long focal length lens is often imperative to recreate reality. Here the subjective factor is as important as the objective. Unless we consciously use distortion for plastic effect, we wish to arouse in those who look at our photographs association with what they already know of the subject and so, by reference to the familiar, to lead them persuasively and convincingly to the unfamiliar. This is that creative plus which we are always hoping we add to photography. Thus if we wish to express tenderness for a mother and her child (as Lewis Hine did in his Ellis Island photographs) we do not want to estrange sympathy by having the resulting picture grotesque, as it will surely be if the baby's head is bigger than the mother's. Or to take another example, suppose you are photographing that extraordinary skyline of downtown Manhattan from the water front, you want to be far enough away from the buildings so that the thousand-foot monsters will be revealed in all their overpowering height. For creative perspective, you must use a long focal length lens and get as far away from your subject as the East River will permit.

Lens Speed

The speed of a lens also enters into the equation. Lenses differ in the amount of light they admit to the film. The more light admitted, the shorter the exposure. This is called speed. Speed is determined by two factors, aperture and focal length. Aperture is the width of the opening in the lens, which is controlled by the diaphragm, a contracting and expanding mechanism. Obviously more light passes through a large opening than through a small. Focal length is the distance light must travel to reach the film after passing through the aperture, intensity of light decreasing with the distance traveled. The rule is that the brightness of the image is inversely proportional to the square of the focal length.

The speed of a lens is measured by the ratio between aperture (aperture being measured for this purpose at the diaphragm's widest opening) and focal length, the resulting factor being called the "f value." If the aperture is 2 inches and the focal length 8 inches, the speed of the lens is expressed as f/4, that is, the focal length (8 inches) is in the ratio of 4:1 to the aperture (2 inches). For a 16-inch lens with an aperture 4 inches in diameter, the ratio is also 4: 1, so that the speed of both lenses is identical. Theoretically, images recorded by both lenses are equally bright and require the same length of exposure. The smaller the f value, the faster the lens; thus f/3.5 is faster than f/6.8.

Depth of Field

When we focus the lens on a given object, objects somewhat nearer the camera and somewhat farther from the camera than the object focused on are also sharp. The distance between the nearest and the farthest objects which appear sharp is called the depth of field. Depth of field depends on focal length, size of aperture and distance of object from the lens. Three simple rules may be stated: (1) the greater the focal length, the less the depth of field; (2) the bigger the opening the less the depth of field; and (3) the farther away the object to be photographed the greater the depth of

24. A RUSHY SHORE, 1886 P. H. EMERSON

Platinum print, from the album
Life and Landscape on the Norfolk Broads.

Museum of Modern Art

25. PEACE: AN ELLIS ISLAND MADONNA, 1905 LEWIS W. HINE

Taken with a 5 x 7 view camera and flash powder
"On a day when 12,000 were crowded through the place."

Courtesy of Corydon Hine

field. Here is another instance of the paradoxical character of photography: long focal length lenses are desirable for the reasons given before, yet they are undesirable because they lack depth of field, to compensate for which it is necessary to stop down the opening and so lose speed in exposure. Or, in regard to aperture, you want the biggest possible opening for maximum speed; then again you sacrifice depth of field. As always, opposing and conflicting forces have to be weighed against each other, in relation to what you want to emphasize most.

"Stops" (the different sizes of the diaphragm) are numbered differently according to the lens. A characteristic series is: f/4.5, f/5.6, f/6.3, f/8, f/11, f/16, f/22, f/32, f/45. The length of time required for exposure at different openings varies directly as the square of the F values. If at f/4 the exposure is 1 second, at f/8 the exposure will need to be 4 seconds, that is, $8^2 : 4^2 :: 64 : 16$, or 4. The relation of one stop to another is in inverse relation to their squares: f/8 is twice as fast as f/11, worked out as follows —$11^2 \div 8^2$ is approximately 2. You do not need to figure out these calculations every time you take a picture, as exposure meters automatically give the length of exposure at different stops. In making calculations, you may consider f/8, f/7.5 and f/7.9 as identical, since film allows for slight variations. Stops control the amount of light passing through the lens. To improve "definition" (or sharpness) of near and far objects focused on at the same time, it is necessary to "stop down" the lens. This is the practical application of the rule that depth of field is less the larger the aperture.

The photographer's creative impulse exercises itself in focusing on the subject in the most effective way. By focusing sharply on a center of interest, you lead the beholder's eye irresistibly to your main theme, directing attention to what is important in your conception of the subject. More, you may deliberately put parts of the picture out of focus to accentuate your main emphasis. An example is a photograph of mine, *Willow Street,* (reproduced in *Graphic Graflex Photography*, p. 161,) in which the iron grille close to the camera is softened so that the three-story house may control the composition. Indeed, it can be argued against the so-called "f/64 school" that its needle-sharp precision of photographic image makes every part of equal interest with every other part and that the eye has no psychological relief from the incessant activity of moving between a number of planes, all equally compelling to the attention. The sense that real objects exist in space and in atmosphere, that they are "round" and solid, is always essential in photography as a pictorial art, because its esthetic appeal from the beginning has been based on the illusion of reality which it manages so successfully to project. Too small stops give almost microscopic sharpness, but lose "roundness" in this sense. The function of the stops here is to enable the photographer to create relations in distance and perspective.

The usefulness of a lens depends on the degree to which it has been "corrected." Correction is necessary because no simple lens will give a completely true image. Common defects are spherical aberration (failure to give sharp images,) chromatic aberration (images blurred by rainbow colors,) and astigmatism (inability to get sharp images of vertical lines with horizontal lines.) Other common faults are curvature of field, coma and distortion. For a detailed analysis of aberrations of lenses, read *Basic Photography*, ¶¶62-69. In the history of lens-making, technological advances have made it possible to eliminate most defects.

In general, aberrations may be corrected by combining lens elements, such as biconvex, plano-convex, convergent meniscus, divergent meniscus, plano-concave and biconcave. An aberration found in one type of element can be neutralized by placing with it another element of opposed type. Air spacing between elements, properties of the glass used, and skillful workmanship unite to make lenses of high quality.

Because the camera eye is a vital point in the whole photographic sequence, your lens can make or break you, photographically speaking. If you use a lens which possesses all the aberrations in an acute degree, you will get results full of distortion—certainly not desirable from a scientific or an esthetic point of view. Every photographer should equip himself with the best lens (or lenses) he can possibly afford—preferably an anastigmatic lens of the convertible type. For quality work, a lens of moderate speed (say f/6.3) is probably to be preferred to a faster lens. With the advance of color photography, both in professional and amateur fields, you will do well to purchase color corrected lenses.

For practical purposes, anastigmatic lenses are the only type which need be considered. They give sharp images with fine definition of straight lines, to the edge of the picture. They are faster than other types. They are corrected for chromatic aberration. And they give uniform definition over the film's entire area when a flat object is photographed parallel to the plane of the film. A lens may be a single unit of one focal length only or a convertible lens, having front and rear elements of unequal focal length, each of which can be used as a separate lens.

Older types of lens are the meniscus and the rectilinear. The meniscus lens is to be found only on cheap box cameras. Because of its great curvature of field, only the center is used. The result is that the lens is slow, its fastest speed usually being 1/15 of a second. The extraordinary depth of field of a meniscus lens (compensation for its slowness) makes it unnecessary to focus the box cameras. Rectilinear lenses represented an advance in lens design when they came into use about 70 years ago. But they are not so highly corrected as anastigmatic lenses and do not possess as great covering power; also they are slower. Built with an element in front and one in back to get straight lines, the rectilinear lens gives beautiful results, if stopping action is not an objective. Atget used a so-called "rapid" rectilinear lens for over 30 years, to make his documents of Paris. By closing down the aperture, he obtained great depth of field and superb definition, though he could not photograph the human activity of Paris and indeed had to rise at dawn to photograph the streets before they filled with traffic.

Wide angle lenses are not another type of lens, but a specialized form designed to cover a wide angle of view, from 50 to 90 or 100 degrees. As a rule a wide angle lens is slow, because it is a short focus lens meant to cover a large plate; therefore it should be used only when the wide angle of view is essential, as in architectural and industrial interiors or panoramic vistas. However, a moderately wide angle lens of 60 or 65 degrees may be had with a speed of f/6.3. Another handicap is that objects close to the lens are distorted, a fault difficult to overcome. Of course, there are instances when distortion is wanted for its own sake and then the wide angle lens comes in handy. Partially to correct the distortion of wide angle lenses, swings are helpful.

Good lenses are plainly marked with the manufacturer's name, focal length, speed and serial number. The manufacturer's name is a guarantee worth heeding; for lens-making is a highly skilled trade, and on the maker's integrity depends the value of the lens you buy. Reliable manufacturers are: Zeiss, Leitz, Goerz, Cooke, Schneider, Voigtländer, Meyer, Dallmeyer,

Bausch & Lomb, Eastman. In buying secondhand lenses, be guided by the reputation of the dealer for fair play.

Lenses, being delicate and costly, require especial care in handling. When not in use, they should be protected with lens caps. For lenses fixed in the camera, only a front cap is necessary. For removable lenses, front and rear caps are needed. Parts should be kept screwed firmly in place, as the air space between elements is an integral factor in a lens' system of refraction. Lenses should not be kept in damp or overheated places, and never in the sun, because of the danger that the Canada balsam with which they are cemented will deteriorate, the lens darkening or its parts loosening. To clean, breathe gently on the lens and polish with a soft old linen cloth.

26. MANHATTAN SKYLINE — Berenice Abbott

Taken with 8 x 10 Century Universal view camera; single element of 9½-inch convertible Goerz Dagor lens; 1/50 second; f/16.

27. FIGHT! CONSUELO KANAGA

Taken with Rolleiflex; 1/200 second; f/11; Superpan Press.

Courtesy of Woman's Day

11. Learning To See: Swings

TO all those who wish to photograph seriously, a word of advice: use a camera with ground glass and adjustments. This may be a small view camera or a hand and stand camera which can be used with or without a tripod and which has flexible swings, like the Deardorff Triamapro. The truth is that adjustments make the camera.

The purpose of adjustments is chiefly to give the camera as nearly as possible the flexibility of the eye. You can look up or down without moving your head, you can see out of the corner of your eye. And you can turn your head up or down to the right or left without moving your body, lying prone, supine or on your side. A camera with swings is similarly almost as flexible.

Normally the lens is centered on the film. The camera, so to speak, looks straight ahead. By means of swings you take the lens off center. You can "point" the view in any direction and yet keep the lens parallel with the film which must be parallel with the object photographed. You cannot do that merely by inclining the camera because then obviously you would get an angular distorted view.

The various types of swings and their uses are explained later in this chapter.

If you want an instrument which will respond to your will and your way of seeing, it is clear that a camera with this adaptability is essential, as I suggested in general terms in Chapter 2.

How does the view camera (or its equivalent among the hand and stand cameras) differ from other ground glass cameras? The bellows extension gives range of sight; by modifications in the focal length from lens to film, it permits of the use of short focal length lenses or of long focal length lenses. The bellows construction gives flexibility of sight so that wide angle lenses may be used; for by pushing up the back of the camera toward the front, the angle of view is cleared; or, on cameras of roughly equal usefulness, the drop bed or swinging bed feature allows the same freedom of action. Thirdly, through swings, sliding front, and rising and falling front, the view camera reaches a subtlety, a flexibility, a plasticity of vision, which is only possible on cameras of this type. Either for correction of distortion, or for distortion for a specific purpose, these adjustments are required.

The view camera is distinguished from other types of cameras by its ground glass on which the image is focused, by the fact that it must be used on a tripod, and by its bellows extension (either double or triple) to permit the use of lenses of varying focal lengths. Focusing may be done either from front or rear, or in some cameras from both front and rear, by racking out the bellows extension by means of pinion screws. Rear focusing is particularly convenient when the bellows are extended to a considerable length, because the photographer can still see the ground glass image without having to make an awkward stretch to the front of the camera. The bellows extension permits the photographer to focus on objects very near or very far away; this makes the view camera useful both for close-up work, such as still life, studio portraits, copying, and for long distance subjects, such as landscapes and city vistas.

For portraits, a stand camera at least 4 x 5 inches is preferred, with a double or triple bellows extension, to enable the operator to set up the camera at a great enough distance from the sitter to obtain a good likeness. There is conspicuous distortion of the "drawing" of features like forehead, nose, cheekbones, jowls, if the camera is placed too close to the person. The use of a longer focal length lens produces a large enough image to allow retouching on the negative and to enlarge easily, without too much grain. Swings and other adjustments are also valuable for correcting distortion in such cases. In portraiture, the eyes are always focused on. If hands, arms, knees, feet, are nearer the camera, the vertical swing can be used to bring them into better focus without closing down the lens, hence saving speed, which is all important for spontaneity of expression.

For architectural or pictorial work, a large view camera should be used, ranging from 4 x 5 up, with all available adjustments, such as rising and falling front, swinging back and front, etc. Architectural photography demands a rising front on the camera, with the preferable addition of vertical and horizontal swings and lateral slides. Without these adjustments, the camera is not able to compensate for optical distortion of vertical and horizontal parallel lines or to take in the vast panorama of modern architecture and construction. It is interesting to note also that Eliot Porter, a Guggenheim fellow for photography, has used a small view camera in his photographs of wild life subjects, certainly not subject matter commonly thought of as being susceptible to conquest by this type of camera. He describes his methods in an article in *U. S. Camera,* No. 8. Paradoxically, the best animal pictures I have seen were made with a view camera, the cats of Thurman Rotan in *U. S. Camera,* No. 2.

A further advantage of the view camera is that its cost is reasonable compared with the cost of good hand and stand cameras, or of the relatively inflexible action cameras, like the 35 mm. or the reflex hand cameras. I have found that metal cameras, however well constructed, are subject to the risk of leaking light around lens board and lens flange. Generally, screws hold more tightly in wood than in metal; therefore wooden cameras do not loosen up so much as all-metal ones. A relatively inexpensive view camera can be used advantageously for still life, portraiture, architectural subjects, copying, pictorial work where fast action is not involved, and for commercial work as a whole, such as fashion work, studio setups, etc.

The arguments in favor of the view camera I developed at length in my chapter in *Graphic Graflex Photography.* However, they may be stated here briefly. The great virtue of the view camera (or its equivalent, like the extremely versatile Deardorff Triamapro, Linhof, or Zeiss Juwel) is that you *see* the picture on the ground glass; you are not shooting in the dark; you are composing, creating your picture as you take it. Obvious faults can be easily and quickly corrected before you take the picture, such as the sun shining in the lens or stray telephone poles intruding in the composition. But a much more subtle reconciliation of elements in nature can also be effected at this time, which would not be possible if you did not see your picture when you clicked the shutter. By using swings and other adjustments, you can bring background and foreground into relation with your center of interest. You can see how both vertical and horizontal parallel lines are distorted and so correct the distortion. You can manipulate the picture in a thousand ways so that the image on the ground glass expresses your sense of the reality and potency of the objective theme. You can even employ the camera's contortions to be your spokesman. Who said the photographer could not control his subject!

For all photographic work where precision and detail are required, where a camera can be set up firmly on a tripod, swings are valuable. In photographing complicated New York City (see my book of 97 photographs, *Changing New York*), I would indeed have been crippled without swings. Cameras for fast action and purely hand work, or cameras from 3¼ x 4¼ down, can scarcely be said to need swings. But from 4 x 5 up, swings on cameras of good design and manufacture are the photographer's salvation. I might add that my photographs, *Stock Exchange, John Watts* and *Night View,* reproduced in this book, are typical of subjects which could only be expressed through the correction made possible by swings.

Swings need thorough familiarity. Such adjustments may be built into a camera and the photographer not even know they are there or how to use them. However, once swings are understood and made use of, no intelligent photographer will do without them. Swings are used to obtain uniform focus when objects focused on are not in the plane of the film. This means that swings can only be used on a ground glass camera. Obviously, you cannot see whether an image is in uniform focus through a view finder or a range finder; only a ground glass, used in the careful manner described in Chapter 3, gives the photographer this sort of advance guarantee that his picture will be in focus and *evenly* in focus. Moreover, so minute are the variations of angle of view, that this uniformity of focus can only be obtained when one factor of the equation remains constant, namely, the camera being fixed at one point in space on a tripod. It is not often that swings would be used while the photographer holds the camera in his hand; but in emergencies it is possible to do so with care and skill.

The advantage of swings is twofold. If the use of a swing, vertical or horizontal or both, can bring more than one plane into focus—which is desirable in itself for technical and esthetic reasons—the lens does not need to be closed down so much, hence there is an increase in speed, a point the desirability of which needs no arguing. Action is saved, difficult shots are made possible. Even if you are in a position where the camera cannot be placed on a tripod, swings will save the day. Suppose you are holding the camera far out over the balustrade of a skyscraper, or over the edge of the Grand Canyon. You can carefully bring the different planes into focus on the ground glass, by using swings. Then an exposure fast enough to permit the camera's being held in the hand is possible, say 1/25 of a second.

Literally, swings mean the swinging back and front. However, practically, they involve all the various adjustments of the view camera and of the flexibly designed hand and stand cameras. These adjustments are listed here in order of complexity and frequency of occurrence. An explanation of their uses follows this listing.

1. *Rising and falling front:* the lens board moves up and down in a plane perpendicular to the ground. This feature is found on many cameras.

2. *Vertical swings:* The lens board or the back of the camera, or both, swing in an arc vertically away from the plane of the subject, to a varying number of degrees, according to the camera. The front swing produces less distortion than the back swing.

3. *Horizontal swings:* the lens board or the back of the camera, or both, rotate in an arc horizontally away from the plane of the subject, to a varying number of degrees, according to the camera. Front swings, either vertical or horizontal, are not found on many cameras.

4. *Lateral slides:* the front standard slides from side to side, perpendicular to the bellows.

5. *Drop bed or swinging bed:* the purpose of this feature is to clear the track for a wide angle lens. The view camera proper achieves the function by another manipulation. In hand and stand cameras of the caliber of the Speed Graphic or the Deardorff Triamapro—the former drop bed and the latter swinging bed with a drop of 30 degrees and an upward tilt of 15 degrees—this adjustment is required to compensate for the fact that the back has no swings. Drop or swinging bed cameras call for a special tripod head.

6. *Revolving back:* a device by means of which a vertical or a horizontal picture may be taken without turning the camera on its side; it pivots in place. In the extremely versatile triamapro, the revolving back (which can be revolved any number of degrees, instead of the right angle 90) can be used to get vertical lines vertical again when the camera has been tilted on a tilting top tripod to correct horizontal distortion.

The following outline is a brief summary of the uses of swings. A more detailed technical analysis is made in Edward J. Cook's two articles, "Swing's the Thing" in *Photo Technique* of July and August, 1940.

1. The rising and falling front is used to include more height and to

exclude undesirable foreground. Instead of raising or lowering the camera, you simply slide the lens board up or down to get what you want into the picture. Even in taking portraits, this is often done.

2. Vertical swings are used to get vertical lines parallel, to get objects in different planes into uniform focus, and to augment the rising front. When the camera is tilted upward and the back adjusted vertically so as to preserve the parallelism of upright lines, the shift in the image is proportional to the tilt given the camera; thus the desired image may be included in the picture, but at the cost of distortion of parallel lines. If the camera is provided with a swing front, the lens board may be aligned parallel to the back. When the lens is parallel to the film, less stopping down is necessary, and there is a resultant desirable gain in speed of exposure. When the lens board is considerably raised, the illumination of the upper corners may fall off. A slight tilt of the front swing rights this.

Swinging front and back are useful for photographing almost every type of subject where great speed is not essential. Obviously, fast action and news photography cannot be done with a camera on a tripod. Otherwise, the alleged disadvantages of the view camera—slowness and complexity—are far outweighed by its advantages in flexibility and control. An example of the usefulness of swings in getting objects in different planes into focus is to be found in portraiture. If the sitter's hands are important, yet you have focused on the eyes as being the center of personality, you can bring both into harmony with a very slight swing. Perhaps you will not bring the hands entirely into focus, but enough into focus so that it will not be necessary to stop down a great deal. I find that the use of the front swing is preferable, if you have it on your camera, because it produces less distortion than the swing back.

3. Horizontal swings perform the same function in the horizontal plane that vertical swings do in the vertical. If you are photographing a row of houses in a narrow street or the top of a table or a desk, swinging the front or back, or both, horizontally will keep horizontal parallel lines from converging too much in the photograph. Acutely diminishing perspective is an optical distortion unpleasant to the eye and should be avoided wherever possible. Swings are the answer to this problem.

4. The lateral slide is particularly useful when the camera must perforce be set up in an awkward position and when adjustment has to be

28. BURNETT HOUSE, LEXINGTON, MISSOURI GAY DILLON

Taken with 4 x 5 Speed Graphic; Zeiss Tessar 5¼ inch lens; 1 second; f/32; medium yellow filter; camera used on tripod; Eastman Supersensitive Pan cut film. Good effects in lighting and in rendering of wood and brick.

29. CITY LANDSCAPE — BERENICE ABBOTT

Deardorff Triamapro; 1/25 second; f/16. Held in hands and swings used. Taken from roof of Irving Trust Company Building at 1 Wall Street, New York.

28. BURNETT HOUSE, LEXINGTON, MISSOURI GAY DILLON

Taken with 4 x 5 Speed Graphic; Zeiss Tessar 5¼ inch lens; 1 second; f/32; medium yellow filter; camera used on tripod; Eastman Supersensitive Pan cut film. Good effects in lighting and in rendering of wood and brick.

29. CITY LANDSCAPE — BERENICE ABBOTT

Deardorff Triamapro; 1/25 second; f/16. Held in hands and swings used. Taken from roof of Irving Trust Company Building at 1 Wall Street, New York.

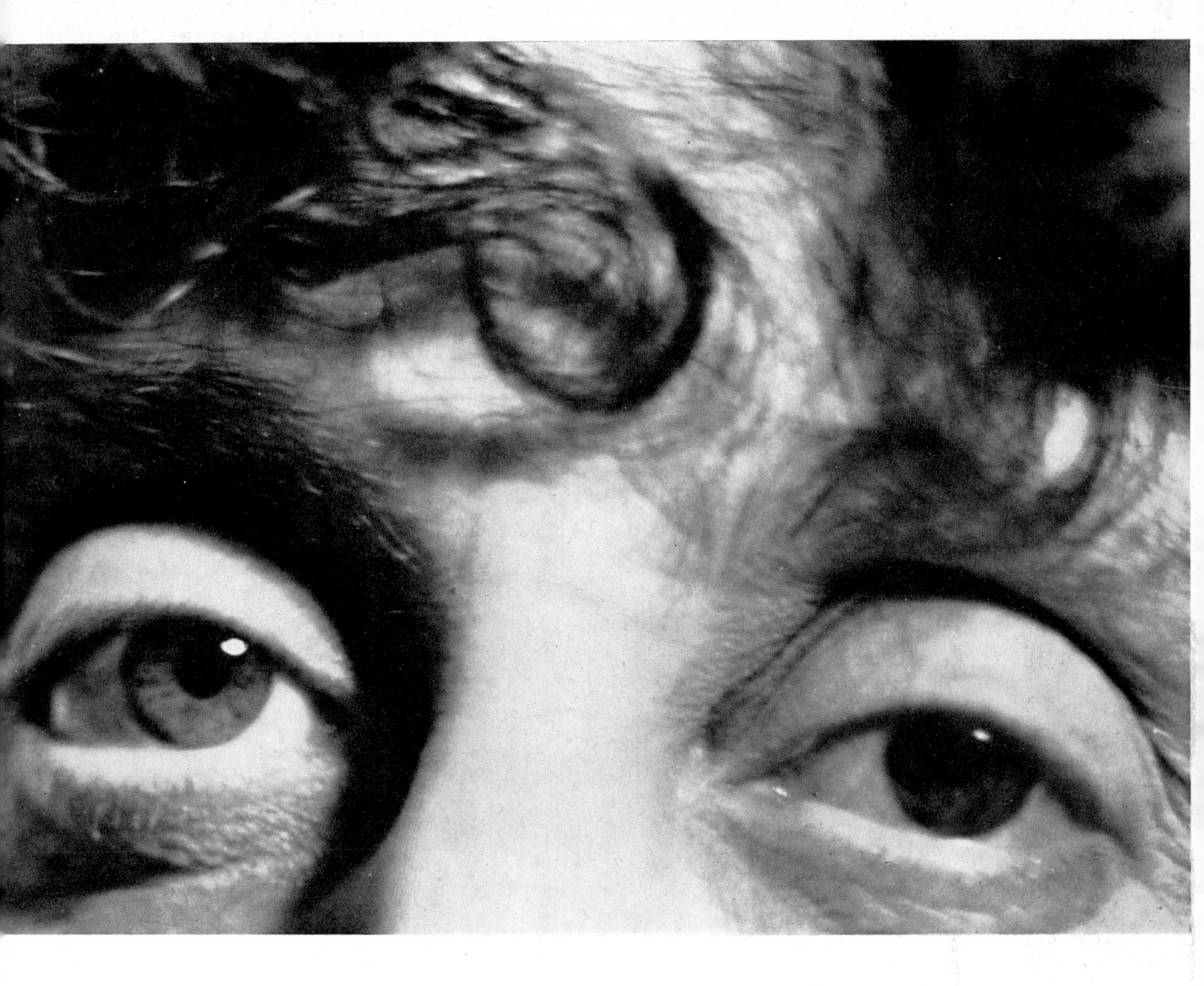

30. EYES OF AUDREY McMAHON — BERENICE ABBOTT

Taken with 5 x 7 reducing back on 8 x 10 Century Universal view camera and photoflood lighting.

31. TRIAMAPRO CAMERA

The most flexible of the American-made hand and stand cameras. The picture illustrates the use of drop bed, rising and falling front, tilting front, lateral slide and lateral swing. The model shown has a focal range finder.

made for its enforced angle of view. With the rising front, vertical and horizontal swings, the lateral slide is used further to correct distortion of horizontal parallel lines, by bringing the lens into a plane parallel to the film.

Study the instructions with your camera. Then practice until you reach for the swings as you do for an auto clutch. Make these manipulations part of your "grooving" for photography, as good form in golf is acquired by creating reflex-like habits. Experiment with and without swings. Take the same subject, using various combinations of adjustments. Think of these parts and their uses not as separate solutions for your problems but as means of achieving solutions which require on your side as well as mechanical familiarity a creative emotion. Unless you see the subject first, you won't be able to force the camera (no matter how subtle and complex) to see the picture for you. But if you have seen the picture with your flexible human vision, then you will be on the road to creating with the camera a vision equivalent to your own. Swings will then really be of value to you.

12. Know Your Materials

THE materials of photography are still primitive, despite great technical progress during its first century. Considering what photography has created as an infant, imagine what can be done when it really grows up, as we hope it will in its second hundred years. Even so, the physical and chemical complexities of the medium are bewildering. Before you go out with a dollar box camera and a roll of film to "take pictures," thousands of scientists and technicians have cooperated to place these relatively simple and inexpensive tools in your hands. Physics and chemistry have been harnessed so that millions may have an absorbing hobby, so that artists, press men and picture-makers of all sorts may employ a new technic.

Science has not solved the mystery of what happens when light strikes light-sensitive silver salts, in the gelatin emulsion. We simply know that the phenomenon occurs. Photography has made use of the fact for diverse purposes. But, although no ultimate answer has been made to the secret of the latent image, manufacturers of photographic materials have pressed science into service in every conceivable way. The photographer, intent on bringing the camera's eye into harmony with his own more vigilant organ, is always demanding faster and faster film, so that he may photograph (if he wish) in utter darkness, as Edgerton has been doing in his stroboscopic experiments at the Massachusetts Institute of Technology. (See *Flash,* in the bibliography.) Or he cries out for a more flexible camera, or lenses of greater speed, or more rigid yet extensible tripods. The gadget trade is one way the photographic millions react to this genuine technological need.

"In photographic factories," writes Clerc in his encyclopedic *Photography: Theory and Practice,* "most elaborate precautions are taken in order to keep the conditions under which the manufacturing processes are carried out absolutely constant, and to avoid all external causes of contamination.

. . . The precautions taken to ensure cleanliness and asepsis are at least as thorough as in the best surgical operating theatres." To make film involves several steps. The light-sensitive emulsion must be coated onto a support, such as a glass plate or film base of celluloid or acetate transparent material. To make the film base itself is an entire operation; a slight change in the equation and TNT would result. The story of how the invention of flexible film base changed photography into a medium for the millions is excitingly told in Taft's chapter on "The Flexible Film" in *Photography and the American Scene.* To manufacture the emulsion is the really delicate part of film-making. Gelatin is mixed with silver nitrate and potassium bromide and iodine, and thoroughly agitated. Next comes ripening or cooking for three hours at 140 degrees Fahrenheit. The material is then shredded and washed. Kept on ice till wanted, the washed shreds are melted and cooked a second time. More chemicals are added; and the emulsion is applied to its base.

A somewhat similar procedure is followed in the manufacture of photographic papers, with different formulas and chemicals used; but the basic principle of light-sensitivity is in operation. For papers, it is necessary to start with pulp, which is transformed into paper, as in an ordinary paper mill. Surfaces and textures are made by different methods, such as calendering and coating. This brief account indicates that photography is by no means a simple affair. Behind the scenes in the factory, science puts in a good day's work before the photographer can take the field for business or for fun.

The kind of film you use depends on what kind of photography you do. If you want to specialize in a given direction, as miniature camera work for medical record, you need to know the technic and materials suited to your especial purpose. Otherwise, you need a general understanding of films, so that you will be able to choose the right kind for whatever work you undertake.

Film is slow, medium and fast, measured by the length of exposure required to obtain a satisfactory negative. Manufacturers are increasing film speed, which is desirable from many points of view. Fast films are usually designated as "super," such as *Superpan* and *Super Plenachrome.* Agfa *Superpan Press, Triple S Pan, Ultra-Speed Panchromatic* and *Super Plenachrome Press,* Eastman *Tri-X* (panchromatic), *Ortho-X, Super Panchro-*

Press, and *Kodak Super-XX,* Defender *Arrow Pan* and *Arrow Pan Press,* and Dupont *Superior 3,* are the fastest films on the market, all with Weston ratings of 100.

The faster the film, the larger the grain; the slower the film, the finer the grain. Grain is not desirable because it shows up in enlargements as pockmarks over the entire print. When action is not important, slower film may be used. In general, the finest grained negatives are produced from orthochromatic film, such as Agfa *Supersensitive Plenachrome.* For this purpose, next in quality are the slower panchromatic films such as Eastman *Panatomic X.* Slower film has greater latitude to permit a range of exposures and generally gives better results than faster film. Where motion does not have to be stopped (as with architectural subjects) medium slow film, such as Eastman *Par Speed Portrait* or *Agfa Portrait Pan* or *Supersensitive Plenachrome,* is best. For commercial work, catalogue subjects and still life, use *Commercial* film. *Process* film is indicated for subjects with extreme contrast between the lightest and darkest parts of the negative. The greatest possible contrast is between black and white, with no intermediate tones. Printed matter, line drawings, maps, lettering, etc., should always be copied with *Process* film.

From the point of view of color sensitivity, there are three kinds of film, "color blind" or regular, orthochromatic and panchromatic. "Color blind" film may be used for photographing black and white subjects, where color values are not important. If the tonal relations of colors are essential to the picture, another type of film must be used, because regular film photographs red and yellow as black instead of the gray which the tone in color appears to the eye. Orthochromatic film is sensitive to more colors than regular film, but it is not sensitive to red, which photographs almost black. If the trade name of a film ends in "chrome," it belongs to the orthochromatic group. Panchromatic film is sensitive to all colors. Thus in the print, red registers as gray in tone instead of black. The prefix "pan" usually designates this type of film.

The intelligent control of color-sensitive film depends on the subject's color values. Such control requires in some instances the use of filters, within the limits discussed in the chapter on that subject, No. 14. Fast, slow and medium speed films come in these three types of color sensitivity. The need for such variety may be illustrated. If we photograph a map with colored lines or letters instead of a black and white map, then we need to use *Panchromatic Process* film with a filter, instead of plain *Process* film. As you experiment, remember that different types of film require different colored safelights during development. Be sure to follow the manufacturer's directions on this point.

A further caution: keep film in a cool, dry place; never in a hot, moist place. Do not pile the boxes or film packs on top of each other, but stack them on their sides.

Paper comes in two weights, single and double. The same emulsion is used for both weights; but the paper support is thinner with single-weight paper, making the cost less. For small prints, single weight paper is easily handled. But for larger prints and enlargements, it is awkward to handle in the solutions. Single weight paper also curls more when drying and is more likely to be damaged and bent than double weight.

Photographic papers come in many colors, ranging from white, natural (off white) and ivory to cream, buff and deep buff. The use of color in photographic prints follows cycles. Whereas a generation ago, buff paper was popular, today it looks old fashioned. The best photographers now see photography as a black-and-white medium and use only white papers, striving more and more for purity and richness of blacks and whites. Nevertheless, there persists a certain vogue for the cream colored papers, which can only be called a hangover from the days of pictorialism, when every effort was made to make a photograph look like anything but a photograph, dressing it up with aquatint effects and following the generally "arty" ideas which prevailed in the graphic art world of the period. The fact is that prints made by etching, wood block printing, lithography or any other traditional graphic art method, were printed on hand made paper which exemplified the standards of craft rather than technology. For a time, during its infancy, photography could not help following the lead of the older black-and-white mediums. Today, it can stand on its own feet and certainly should do so in these subtle matters of taste and esthetic appeal.

Surfaces and textures of paper play an integral part in printing. Here, personal taste will be a factor. But the choice of a surface or a texture should largely be determined by the type of photograph you desire to make. Some papers are smooth, some rough. Some are shiny ("glossy"), some are dull ("matte") in finish. Between the two lies "semimatte," a pleasing velvety surface. Paper with a slightly uneven surface or "tooth," such as Eastman *P.M.C.* 11 or Agfa *Brovira Royal,* is good for enlarging because the grain of the enlarged negative is "absorbed" by the grain of the paper. For big enlargements where minute detail is not essential, as in my portrait of Orozco (Pl. 33) where I wished somewhat to soften his beard, a rough paper is best. On the other hand, for a group of people where the heads are small, too much detail is lost on a rough paper, and a smoother surface is to be preferred, as in Ansel Adams' photograph here reproduced.

Papers imitating the surface of canvas or the texture of "old masters" are much too "arty" for the straightforward medium of photography. In fact, trying to make a photograph look like an etching is just as bad as the fallacy in architecture of building a skyscraper with steel frame construction and then covering up the basic form with pseudo-Gothic ornament. Let the medium speak for itself, frankly as what it is, the twentieth century picture making art.

Aside from papers like these which are anathema, whether you use a dull surface or a surface with a slight sheen is a matter of taste. But most prints need a little "spotting," and matte paper conceals marks of retouching better than shinier surfaces. Another practical consideration has to do with reproduction. Blacks appear blacker the shinier the paper, looking blackest on glossy paper. Glossy paper is therefore used for prints for magazine or newspaper reproduction. Some very good photographers use glossy paper for their finished exhibition prints, in fact. As a rule, more detail is registered on smooth than on rough paper. Hence, the vogue among the younger documentary photographers for prints on glossy paper, because precise detail is picked out and emphasized.

Besides brand names, like *Azo, Haloid, Brovira, P.M.C.,* etc., paper comes in degrees of contrast, known as "grades." Generally, grades are classified by numbers, surfaces by letters. For example, *Azo F2* equals "*Azo* glossy, normal contrast," while *Azo E5* means "*Azo* semimatte, very contrasty." The usefulness of grades is discussed in Chapter 17, "The Art of Printing."

Paper, like film, should be kept in a cool place. Unlike film, it should not be stored in too dry a place, as paper so stored has a tendency to crack.

From the chemical point of view, there are three types of paper—bromide, chloride and chlorobromide. Bromide paper has the fastest emulsion.

32. BATTERY CHICKENS — Berenice Abbott

Taken with 9 x 12 cm. Linhof; 1/100 second; f/16; 2 flash bulbs;
Agfa Superpan Press film pack. Used swing back
to get planes in focus.

Life Magazine

33. JOSE CLEMENTE OROZCO: NEW YORK, 1936 — BERENICE ABBOTT

Taken with 5 x 7 reducing back on 8 x 10 Century Universal view camera; 48 cm. single element of convertible Zeiss Protar lens; 1 second; f/16; Supersensitive Panchromatic; photoflood lighting.

It is chiefly used for the slower enlargers and is often called "projection paper." Its emulsion is closest in character to that of film, which also contains potassium bromide. This fact makes it necessary to handle bromide papers under a dim safelight, Series OA being suitable. Chloride paper has a much slower emulsion than bromide paper and can be used under a stronger safelight. It is a "contact" paper, so called because the paper is in direct contact with the negative. It is sometimes called "gaslight paper" because gaslight was used for printing before electrical illumination was invented or perfected. Instead of potassium bromide, sodium chloride is used in its manufacture. This type of paper gives a greater degree of contrast than does bromide paper; hence contact prints are usually more brilliant than enlargements. Chlorobromide paper is a combination of the two types above described. It is of medium speed, measured by the sensitivity to light. It is used both for contact printing and for enlarging; but the source of light for enlarging must be much stronger than for bromide paper. For extremely contrasty negatives, a paper such as Eastman *Illustrators Special* makes excellent contact prints.

To achieve technical perfection, as a means to more complete expressiveness, the photographer must not only know film and paper, but he must make a habit of good laboratory technic. The "don'ts" and "musts" which sound so formidable are really a simple matter if you start your photographic life right. Sloppiness and dirtiness from bad working methods cause so much grief that a little thought and time at the beginning are more than repaid.

The water used for photographic solutions is of prime importance. Rust from pipes is a harmful substance. If you use tap water, a filter such as the Elkay Photo-Pure Water Filter, selling for $3.15, is advisable. If you can use distilled water for all solutions, that is to be preferred. Failing these precautions, make sure of the relative purity of water by boiling it and allowing sediment to settle.

Ordinary commercial chemicals will not do for photographic purposes. Use only the purest products. Among others, Agfa, Eastman and Mallinckrodt are reliable. Excepted from this rule is hydrochloric acid, used for cleaning bottles and graduates. It may be purchased in the commercial grade, commonly known as muriatic acid.

Chemicals cannot be expected to act satisfactorily unless they are properly taken care of. This means proper storage. Some solids, such as hypo crystals, which do not deteriorate easily, come in cardboard boxes or in bags. But very few chemicals used in photography can be stored in this manner for a long period of time. Generally speaking, all chemicals should be kept in containers, such as bottles or boxes, tightly stoppered or covered so that dust and dirt cannot enter. It is even more important that the containers be airtight so that oxygen is excluded; for oxidization makes the chemicals unusable. Since many chemicals are deliquescent, that is, absorb moisture from the surrounding atmosphere, it is essential to keep them in a dry storage place. Excessive heat is also to be avoided.

Bottles for the storage of solutions should be immaculately clean. To clean bottles, fill them nearly to the top with water. Add a small amount of hydrochloric (muriatic) acid, say about three ounces for a quart bottle, taking care to keep acid from splashing on hands or in face. Let stand for half an hour or so. Shake well. Then rinse. Stubborn stains may require the use of a bottle brush. A further word of caution: always add the acid to the water, don't add water to the acid.

Precision is essential in photography. In measuring chemicals, there must be no "baker's dozen," no added pinch of salt, no sugar thrown in with a lavish hand. The formula must be followed meticulously. Hence the need for a good scale. The type commonly used for weighing solid chemicals is the studio scale, designed to weigh small quantities from one grain to four ounces and fifty grains. Paper spoons are handy to ladle chemicals from their containers to the scale. At all times, when not in use, the scale should be left in a state of balance, that is, the slide on the graduated beam should be brought back to zero and the weights removed from the pan.

Next comes order of mixing. Chemicals must be dissolved in the sequence stated in the formula. Developer should be mixed at the temperature recommended, usually not above 125 degrees Fahrenheit. If this rule is not strictly followed, the developer will be colored instead of clear, or the solution may produce fog or even a white sludge on films. Each chemical must be completely dissolved before the next is added. If this is not done, discoloration of the solution results, making it unfit for use. Stir constantly while adding dry chemicals to the water.

Stock solutions are concentrated solutions to be diluted with various proportions of water at the time of using. Bottles containing stock solutions should be carefully labeled as to the amount of dilution required, i.e., 1: 2 or 1: 4, meaning one part of stock solution to two parts of water or four parts, as may be. Bottles must be kept full and be tightly stoppered. For this reason, small sizes (quarts, pints or even half pints) are desirable.

Developing solutions need four kinds of chemical substances: developing agents, accelerators, preservatives and restrainers. Developing agents change the exposed silver salts of film or paper to metallic silver. The commonly used developers (or "reducers") are pyro, hydroquinone, metol, elon and amidol. Accelerators are just that, substances added to accelerate chemical action; for most developers require the addition of an alkali in order to become active. The more alkaline the developing solution, the more rapid and vigorous its action. If the alkali is omitted, the solution will not work. The accelerators usually used are sodium carbonate, sodium hydroxide, potassium hydroxide, borax and "kodalk." If a preservative is not added, developers react to the oxygen in the air and become useless, discoloration revealing the fact. Sodium sulphite is used for this purpose in nearly all formulas. Restrainers prevent the developer from acting on the unexposed silver particles, which would cause fog. In printing, the restrainer helps keep the whites clear, giving the finished print more snap. The most successful formulas are those recommended by the makers of the film and paper you decide to use. All manufacturers supply booklets of their formulas free of charge.

In printing *only*, the intermediate rinse between developer and hypo serves as a check bath, to stop further development, by neutralizing the alkali in the developer. This keeps the print from staining and prolongs the hypo's life. Acetic acid is used for this purpose, as is explained in Chapter 8.

The acid fixing bath (hypo) dissolves out from the emulsion unused silver salts, whether in negative or print. Hypo also hardens the film's gelatin. Basic actions and agents of the acid fixing bath are: (1) weak acetic acid, to stop development and eliminate stains; (2) a hardening agent, such as potassium alum, to harden the gelatin (already softened by the developer's sodium carbonate) so that it will not swell during washing; and (3) the preservative sodium sulphite, to prevent developer carried over into the fixing bath on negatives or prints from turning them brown. Hypo must be handled carefully. Do not mix a larger quantity than you can use in a week's time. In very hot weather, hypo should be mixed fresh for each use. Temperatures above 85 degrees ruin the fixing bath, causing a pale yellow precipitate to form.

The final washing should remove all residue of the fixing bath. Washing must be thorough to insure permanence in film and print.

Neglect to maintain proper temperatures in developers is one of the most common forms of carelessness. Very cold developer is relatively inactive and increases the length of time of development. Cold solutions produce contrasty negatives, which lack shadow detail. A too warm solution is erratic in action, increases size of grain and produces dense negatives.

Do not be too economical with developer or hypo. When developer is wearing out, it becomes slower in action, brownish in color and frothy. Hypo becomes cloudy, whereas it should be clear, to do its work efficiently. Replace solutions when these danger signals appear.

34. FAMILY PORTRAIT — Ansel Adams

Made with Leica. This fine group portrait illustrates the practical point about enlarging small heads onto glossy paper to bring out all possible detail in the small negative.

Courtesy of Carl Zeiss, Inc.

35. TREE ROOTS EUGÈNE ATGET

Taken with 18 x 24 cm. view camera; rapid rectilinear lens; glass plate.

Collection of Berenice Abbott

13. Problems of Exposure

EXPOSURE is the issue on which photography splits into two camps. There are the "optimists" who follow the "minimum" school of analysis, exposing for detail in the high lights, and there are the "pessimists" who follow the "maximum" school, exposing for detail in the shadows. My own conviction is that overestimating length of exposure is to be preferred to underestimating. Photography used to be called "shadow catching." Surely, the subtle and less easily seen truths hidden in shadow are as organically part of the picture as brilliant accents of white.

The negative is the link between subject and print, therefore indispensable. To produce a good negative is the photographer's first task. Technically, a good negative depends on correct relation between exposure and development. But since film cannot be developed until it has been exposed, exposure is the stage of the process where creation of a good negative begins. Correct exposure is essential for success in photography. The reason is inherent in the chemical nature of the process. Under a microscope, minute particles of silver bromide are seen to be scattered through the emulsion. Each tiny grain undergoes chemical change when light strikes the film. The action is not at once visible, but becomes evident when the exposed particles turn to black metallic silver in the developer. To provide enough light to bring about this change, and yet not too much, is the purpose of exposure calculations. For the recording of tones on sensitive film depends not only on the strength of the light which strikes the film but also on the length of time light acts on the silver salts.

When we photograph a house, it reflects different amounts of light. Some parts of the house reflect direct rays from the sun, while parts in shadow reflect indirect light. The bright area reflecting direct light creates a high light, the dark area a shadow. Between high lights at one end of the scale and shadows at the other, there are many gradations, called tones. The problem of photography is to reproduce in black and white the exact tones of a subject; for by variations in brightness, we express form and color in the two dimensional black-and-white print.

Fortunately there is some latitude in film emulsions between minimum time required to affect the silver particles and maximum time. Outside this range, a longer exposure blackens so many of the silver particles that the tones at the black end of the scale darken too much and no difference can be seen between them. This is overexposure. Both shadows and high lights print gray and intermediate tones are dull. An overexposed negative is dense, flat, gray and often streaked and uneven. If the film has been underexposed, not enough silver particules are changed by the light's action and the negative is thin, with the result that shadows merge into each other, print too black, have no detail. Also, intermediate tones are not in correct relationship or may not be present at all, so that the photograph looks like a silhouette.

Since a good negative is the first step toward good photography, exposure must be calculated carefully, taking into account all the factors which affect the lighting of your subject. Strength of light cannot be judged accurately by the eye alone. Three elements influence it, time of day and year, place, and weather, besides the constantly changing character of sunlight itself. At midday the sun is stronger than in the morning, no matter how bright slanting rays at 7 a.m. or 5 p.m. may *seem*. Obviously, it is much stronger in summer than in winter. Geographical location, that is, distance from the equator, also controls strength of light. Clouds, fog, rain, snow, complicate the light question further.

In judging the strength of light, remember that apparent brilliance does not mean strong light. Light may be strong on a cloudy summer day. Therefore, don't be afraid to work on a day which is not sunny. Many subjects are ideal when the light is weak or when there is a slight veil over the sun. Architectural details, such as doorways, are better in a diffused light.

The second factor which controls exposure is the color of your subject. Learn to classify subjects according to color, because colors reflect varying amounts of light. A white horse reflects more light than a black horse, and a field of snow more than a dark cliff. In winter, when people are dressed in dark clothes, a street scene presents another problem than in summer, when they dress in light colored clothes.

Speed of film is the third factor. Film differs in the length of exposure required. At first, use the same kind of film all the time. Also, work with film which is not too fast, such as *Plenachrome* or *Panatomic X*. Be sure you know the speed rating of the film you use.

Lens speed also enters the equation. Given the same amount of light reflected by the same object, a shorter exposure is needed with a fast lens than with a slow lens. Aperture is another variable. The larger the opening through which light enters, the shorter the exposure. The rule is: exposure varies with the square of the stops, or f/4 is to f/8 as 16 is to 64, i.e., 4. The smaller opening (f/8) requires an exposure four times as long as the larger opening (f/4), other things being equal. However, you should keep in mind that there is a loss of depth of field when the larger apertures are used. Here, as always in photography, you weigh a gain against a loss and make your decision on the basis of what quality is most important to you in a given situation. In photographing action subjects, such as skaters in leaps off the ice, you may wish to show the figures in midair and let the background take care of itself. Then the larger aperture is the right one for you.

With all these factors to harmonize, how can you ever decide correct exposure? No one can take time to figure out the exposure for each subject by tables of coefficients, as used to be done. But every one can use one of the meters, calculators or other guides on the market today. Refer back to Chapter 3 for recommendations on this point. With any exposure aid, you must learn to use your own judgment. No meter, calculator or other device can do the work for you. It can give you a minimum exposure. With that as a basis, you adapt the exposure to conditions as you understand them. For normal exposure, it is always safe to double the time given. When you use a meter, test the darkest shadow or area in which you want to show detail. Thus you will guard against too "optimistic" a reading.

One more warning: meters are fragile instruments for precise measurements; so handle them gently. Do not drop them or bang them about. Above all, do not expose them to extreme heat or leave them in the sun or light when not in use.

Calculating Correct Exposure

As there is no one camera for all purposes, so there is no one standardized time and aperture at which all photographs can be taken. Every picture differs from every other; its successful making combines many elements. The vast majority of negatives are underexposed, that is, sufficient light has not reached the sensitive emulsion to produce chemical change. Hence, the picture is but a pale ghost of what you saw and hoped to recreate in your photograph.

There are many reasons for the gap between hope and performance. Speed of film is usually exaggerated. Shutters, even the best, are often inaccurately timed. The listed aperture of a lens only holds true when it is focused on infinity. Thus, a lens of f/8 speed may actually operate at f/11 or f/16 when focused on an object near the camera. The real speed is the distance from the lens to the film in focus, divided by the diameter of the aperture. For example, take a 9½ inch lens with a diameter of 1⅜ inches which has a speed of f/6.8 when focused on infinity, approximately, 100 feet. The same lens, with the same aperture, when focused to take a portrait at 9 feet, has a speed of only f/7.8, a figure obtained by dividing the diameter (1⅜ inches) into the distance from lens to film in focus, which is 10½ inches for the portrait at 9 feet. Related to this variable factor of difference in lens speed when used at different distances is the decrease in speed caused by using a longer bellows extension. Furthermore, lenses rated at the same speed may vary according to the number of elements, surfaces, cementing, brilliance of glass. Finally, perhaps the most important reason for the difficulties photographers encounter in making correct exposure is that they are tempted only too frequently to expose for high lights alone.

The first rule to emphasize is: expose for the shadows. Determine the darkest area in which you want detail. If you are using a meter, take your reading from this area; if a *Wellcome Calculator*, use the area's estimated darkness in your calculations. If your meter is of the photoelectric cell type, hold it close enough so that only light from that specific area registers. In other words, hold your meter as close to the subject as the diameter of the area, whether six inches or six feet. That is, if the area you are testing is the side of a house, about 20 feet will be a reasonable distance to hold the meter; if a row of books in dark colored bindings, perhaps 10 inches away will do. Be careful not to cast a shadow with your hand or body.

In applying the rule of exposing for the shadows, you naturally will not use the meter on excessively dark detail unimportant to the finished picture. If you do not want such detail, you will be wise to suppress it entirely by "underexposing" the unwanted area. "Expose for the shadows and let the high lights take care of themselves" is practically always true. But there are exceptions. If your subject is a snow-covered field brilliantly lit by sun with shadows comparatively unimportant, it would be a mistake to expose for shadow detail. Or if a large section of the picture is sky, too full an exposure for the foreground would surely overexpose the sky, and its effect would be lost.

After you have determined the correct exposure, remembering to double the minimum time indicated by meter or calculator, you will have to learn to vary the amount of time slightly, according to the degree of contrast shown in the subject. To explain contrast in this context, we may give a very elementary example. A black cat and a white rat together present extreme contrast; a gray mouse and a maltese cat very little. In more subtle and complicated relations, contrast pervades the world of pictures, whether in black and white or in color. For normal subjects, having a moderate degree of contrast between high lights and shadows, use "normal exposure," or twice the *minimum* time estimate. For subjects with great contrast between light and dark areas, use slightly longer exposure ("plus exposure"), one stop larger than normal exposure. For subjects with little difference between light and dark tones, use a slightly shorter exposure ("minus exposure"), one stop smaller than normal exposure.

Subjects of high contrast, requiring plus exposure, include interiors, indoor portraits, subjects under trees but with sunlight rays and sky, very bright landscapes with heavy shadows or dark objects in the foreground, snow scenes with black trees in the foreground. Subjects of medium contrast, requiring normal exposure, are average street scenes and ordinary sunlit landscapes with even distribution of light and shade. Subjects of low contrast, requiring minus exposure, include open landscapes, ordinary landscapes on a dull day, open air portraiture in the shade. A caution: do not photograph people in direct sunlight. If you must, watch the shadows and give plus exposure. Brightly lighted subjects with important shadows require plus exposure. You might think that a subject in bright light needs less exposure than one in shadow. However, bear in mind that the brighter the sun the darker the shadows, hence the need for adequate exposure to produce details in the shadows.

Subjects in weak light with no pronounced shadows require minus exposure. Since such subjects (called "flat") do not have strong shadows, overexposure is bad because it exaggerates their flatness. Why photographs taken in a weak light or under a haze require minus exposure may be explained by an example. If you photograph a house with a front porch, the high lights on a sunny day will be bright and the shadows dark. To show detail, you need plus exposure. But if the light is weak or hazy, the high lights will not be brilliant and the shadows will be gray. Contrast is less; therefore, to preserve the range of tones, minus exposure is necessary.

Since contrast is also affected by development, keep in mind the fact that overexposure and underdevelopment "flatten" the negative, in other words bring the tones closer together. Conversely, too short exposure and too long development tend toward harshness or excessive contrast. Thus, the production of a good negative depends on the length of time it is developed as well as on the length of time it is exposed. When a film goes into the developer, all the silversalts acted on by light begin to darken. But those acted on by the most light darken faster than those acted on by a medium amount of light, and parts in shadow which reflected the least light develop most slowly. At first, all the tones are close together. But the longer the negative stays in the developer, the greater the contrast between dense parts which produce high lights and thin parts which produce shadows.

Many people tend to overdevelop their films. Aim to develop so that the contrast between high lights and shadows is not so great but that both extremes can be printed satisfactorily on normal grade printing paper. Such balancing of tonalities is part of the intelligent control of photography (that improvement on nature which is the goal of all art) which enables the photographer to minimize or even to eliminate undesirable effects. By the relations he creates, he makes the photograph a creative statement, not merely that "literal scientific transcript of nature" which P. H. Emerson believed photography to be. To this end, develop a critical attitude toward your negatives. Study them to detect the causes of failure or success. Record in a notebook time of day, light conditions, film used, length of

36. HUDSON RIVER VALLEY MARGARET BOURKE - WHITE

Wardhaven Hall at Watervliet with Hugh Campbell, age 7, adding a little human interest to characteristic Americana of the region.

Life Magazine

37. AGROBIOLOGY BERENICE ABBOT

Taken with 9 x 12 cm. Linhof; 1 second; f/16; natural daylight. Used swing back to get planes into focus. Normal exposure was needed to give quality of growing peas in sand. Enlargement of a part of the negative.

Life Magazine

38. BARN NEAR PULASKI, TENN., 1935 BERENICE ABBOTT

Taken with 8 x 10 Century Universal view camera; 12-inch Zeiss Protar lens; 1/25 second; f/16; K2 filter.

39. COUNTRY ROAD — EUGÈNE ATGET

Taken with 18 x 24 cm. view camera; rapid rectilinear lens; glass plate.
Original print on gold chloride paper. No filter was used.
See Chapter 15 for application of edge spacing.

Collection of Berenice Abbott

exposure, and stop used. Compare the finished negative with these data to discover what factor, if any, was erroneously calculated.

When studying your subject for exposure, observe color from a photographic point of view. Discrimination can be cultivated by comparing your final print with the subject itself. One thing to keep in mind: do not choose as a subject a pretty red barn or a bright red fire engine because the color allures you. Unless the subject's form and line are interesting in themselves, they are not photogenic. The picture must compose in graphic terms. By half closing your eyes and squinting at the subject, you get a good idea of its black-and-white values.

In closing, the excellent summary called "Golden Rules for Exposure" of *Basic Photography* may be quoted here. These rules should be found engraved in every photographer's heart.

1. Expose for the shadows.
2. Develop for the high lights.
3. Expose fully for a strong, brightly lighted subject.
4. Avoid too full exposures with flat subjects.
5. Weak light and haze are usually equivalent to a flat subject.
6. Too much exposure and too little development gives flatness.
7. Too much development and too little exposure gives harshness.
8. Observe the color of the subject from a photographic color point of view.
9. Always exercise good judgment in classifying the subject.
10. Note the distance from the camera to the object to be photographed.
11. Do not forget that the light and shade contrasts are the most important parts of the picture.
12. Do not put too much faith in the speed ratings of a shutter.
13. When in doubt overexpose, and if several exposures are made in order to be sure of a good negative increase one exposure over another by at least 50 per cent.
14. Remember that in the early morning or in the late evening the light is frequently yellow or even red and therefore it is less strong, so far as ordinary plates or films are concerned, than it is during the middle of the day.
15. Do not use a larger stop than is necessary.

14. Use and Misuse of Filters

LIGHT from the sun, which we call "white," is made up of visible light rays—red, yellow, green, blue and violet, seen in the spectrum—and invisible light rays—infra-red and ultra-violet. Pass a beam of light through a prism, and you will refract it so that the colors of the spectrum are visible. The light we speak of so frequently in photography is composed of all these colors or light waves. The catch is that they differ in strength, depending on the length of the light wave. This difference in strength results in unequal registering of light, which brings us to filters.

Filters are colored transparent discs, preferably of optical glass, which are placed in front of or behind the lens. Filters are of two kinds, correction and contrast. Correction filters are used to compensate for the difference in strength of light of different colored subjects, while contrast filters are used to accentuate the black-and-white values of subjects so that the tonal relations will be harmonious with the tonal relations existing between the colors themselves. With correction filters, strong rays from the ultra-violet end of the spectrum are held back, which would otherwise overexpose the negative. Then the light reflected from greens, yellows and reds has a chance to register in the negative, while excessively strong light from the brightest areas—sky, snow, water—is partially or wholly "absorbed" by the filter. Thus, the extreme range of tones in nature is equalized to bring the natural tones into the photographic emulsion's scale of tones.

Filters are like many other beautiful gadgets—something to beware of. I write this knowing that many epithets will be hurled at me. After all, filters look pretty, they are nice to handle. If a photographer be permitted an occasional sleepless night from excitement over a brand-new camera, why not with many other lovely gadgets? (Crotchets sounds very much the same to me. What was it De Quincey wrote? "He ruined himself and all that trusted him by crotchets that he could never explain to any rational man.") Surely now the making of lovely pictures will be a snap. Alas, all I can say is *Beware!* More than likely these beautiful filters will prevent you from making lovely pictures and only add to your bewilderment. (Do I hear some one murmur, "Befilterment"?)

Advice is cheap and I don't like to lay down—nor can I—rigid laws for photography. Photography is a big loose behemoth, a Gargantua, a Gulliverian Brobdingnag, which needs pruning, simplification, more science, but especially more common sense. As far as amateurs are concerned, I want to say unequivocally that you can get along very well with one filter, medium yellow if you use orthochromatic film or yellow-green if you use panchromatic, and use that only when really necessary.

The only kind of filter worth buying is one with color incorporated in the glass, built to fit securely and flatly over the lens. In addition to the disadvantage that a filter materially increases the length of exposure, it can detract from the perfection of the negative if it is not free from dust and fingermarks and/or not absolutely parallel to the lens.

When can you safely work without a filter? Certainly in most miniature camera work, particularly if you use the miniature camera for the purposes for which it was intended and which it serves superbly—candid work under poor lighting conditions. In such work, you are not after gray skies, fleecy clouds, tonal quality; you want human interest, action, expression. What is more, the use of a filter complicates your work and delays it, may even prevent you from getting those perfect negatives so necessary with tiny films. Naturally, this does not apply to specialized technical or scientific work with the miniature camera in which color correction is essential, as in making a medical record of skin diseases with Kodachrome. Nor does it apply to color photography, generally.

There is a tendency in our country to overemphasize skies, to dramatize them, to make them so dark that they weigh heavily, heavily, on the sight. Where is that sensation of light, or expanding universe, which can be so thrilling in a photograph? Why the incessant stress on dreary, heavy, dark, black skies? We may even go back to subject matter itself. Can skies be properly photographed until color photography is vastly improved? I have yet to see a cloud picture which is as good as the cloud itself. Where is the delicacy, the flight of space? Why aim the lens at the sky and ignore the earth, with its deep rooted, teeming, human, man-made civilization? Are there dark, lurking philosophical reasons? In any case, to get a reasonably good sky effect, the foreground or earth must be sacrificed. Granted, reluctantly, that personal taste rules here, I'll take the earth.

A further point is that even without a filter, fairly good skies are possible. At the most logical times to take pictures, when the light is good and shadows are long enough to give good form, that is, mornings and afternoons, light is yellower than at midday. As the rays slant more, light even becomes reddish, acting as a filter itself. Many beautiful cloud effects can thus be made without a filter, by studying the varying character of natural light and taking advantage of its changing characteristics. For general outdoor subjects, where skies do not need a tone or where important whites (such as white sails or white buildings) do not stand out against a blue sky, filters are unnecessary. To prove the point, take a series of pictures with a filter and without, and compare results.

You do need to use a filter if a third or more of your picture is sky, snow, water, sand or other surface of similar reflecting power. If it is more pleasing to have a tone over your sky than to have it blank white, then a filter is needed. Around the seashore or other large bodies of water where powerful light is reflected from water, sand, and everywhere, a filter is necessary.

In the above, the discussion has had to do with the use of filters for correction, so that the relative value of colors will be registered as understood by the eye. Contrast filters are used to distort the values registered in the negative, when it is necessary to over correct a color value. To appear lighter in the print, a color should be photographed through a filter of its own color. For example, if you photograph bright red cherries in an emerald green bowl without using a filter, both cherries and bowl will appear gray and flat. The cherry-bowl combination needs to be taken with a red filter if you want the cherries to register high in key. To appear darker, a color should be photographed through a filter which absorbs that color. For example, a woman in a bright blue dress should be photographed with a red filter if it is desired to have the dress seem almost black. Generally, blue appears dark through a red filter, so that skies may be darkened by this means, or blueprints may be photographed as black.

For commercial and scientific work, a more complicated use of filters may be necessary. In some cases, special machines, such as the General Electric recording spectral photometer, are even used. In all, there are a hundred or more filters. Eastman Kodak Co. publishes a book, *Wratten Light Filters,* which describes their many uses.

Contrast filters are used frequently for commercial work, particularly furniture photography. Oak and similar woods with grain are definitely improved in rendering by using a deep yellow contrast filter. With contrast filters, you need to know which filters to use to photograph given colors light and dark. The most commonly used contrast filters are yellow, orange, red and green. Yellow is used for general correction. Deep yellow is used in telephotography to cut out haze; also for furniture, and for general contrast. Red is used to photograph mahogany furniture; to photograph blue as black as in blueprints; to reproduce reds very light; *it is never used with orthochromatic film.* Green is used to photograph purple or violet type-written letters; to render green light and red dark.

Filters are only used with color-sensitive film, that is, orthochromatic or panchromatic. Two filters cannot be used together. The precise filter factor should be noted on your filter case, this having been carefully calculated by consulting a reliable reference like *Photo-Lab-Index.* Remember, further, that the same filter may have different factors when used with different films.

15. Composition

WHAT do we mean by composition? The word, signifying orderly arrangement, is generally misunderstood and misused, even as composition itself is. Some photographers ignore composition entirely. Some are afraid of it as "art," a distant goal difficult to attain. Some give the word exaggerated importance. For the latter, composition is an end in itself, separated from subject matter and meaning. They come to believe that if a picture has a good "composition," that is all it needs. This is not true. Composition *without* subject matter is unthinkable in any real sense. Composition is not an abstract quantity separable from its parts. It is integral, as closely tied up with the body of the picture as veins and muscles are articulated with the human body. Composition without content cannot be imagined.

What, then, is the function of composition in the pictorial arts? Without composition, a picture lacks eloquence, we say. But more than that, without composition the picture cannot speak at all. Composition is the formal method by which we organize the unrelated objects and incidents of real life into the unity of art. It is a device of language designed to communicate meaning to those who read the language—in this case, pictorially, through the eyes. To be articulate and intelligible in any medium—and it is appropriate here to link photography with the spoken and written communication made by words—you need grammar and syntax. Otherwise your effort to communicate a thought, an idea, an emotion, will fail, whether visual or verbal. You can put one word after another, and say nothing, unless you use these words (comparable to visual images in the pictorial arts) within a framework of familiar acceptance. This does not mean that language is frozen into conventions. The great artist is always breaking the conventions and creating new ones. But he does so usually by reference to the old as the point of departure toward the new.

40. ORPHAN LEWIS W. HINE

Taken with 5 x 7 view camera. An excellent composition.
For detailed analysis, see text.

Courtesy of Corydon Hine

41. BETHLEHEM, PA., 1936 WALKER EVANS

Taken with 8 x 10 Deardorff view camera; 36 inch Zeiss Protar; 5 seconds; f/45; Agfa Supersensitive Panchromatic. Contact print.

Courtesy of the Farm Security Administration

In the picture-making medium of photography, a visual grammar and syntax is as much needed as grammar and syntax are needed in verbal language. In other words, arrangement or organization of lines and of areas of light and shade is necessary if the picture is fully to express its meaning. Composition, therefore, is a method of creating meaning. If composition is defined as a method of saying what you want to say most effectively, the definition implies that you have something to say. There are "artists" in all mediums who have nothing to say, but are very elegant in their use of language, whether words, paint, music or what. Photography, by its very realistic and factual nature, permits the artist to lie less than many other mediums. To be sure, the photographic process may be manipulated in ways that seem to deny photography's realistic character. But these diversions do not continue to hold attention as do photographs in the great tradition of Brady, Hill, Nadar and Atget.

To be sure, whatever the tradition, there will always be those whose splendid rhetoric rings out, as through an amplifier, who yet say nothing—as in the famous nonsense speech with which Chaplin's *Modern Times* opens. Among the many subjects chosen for exploitation by these photographic rhetoricians have been the fad for "pictorialism," like the old-time photographers who spent all their energies imitating painters soft and fairylike; the fad for female beauties *ad infinitum,* as in the so-called "art" magazines; the fad for dramatic lighting in a theatrical mood; the fad for uncalled-for trick "angle shots"; the fad for "print quality" for its own sake. Thus in photography, as in any other language, the "words" which can be used to say something important and immediate can also be distorted and robbed of meaning.

Composition has been defined as the most effective way of saying what you want to say. To produce the effect you want—documentary, realistic, esthetic, social—you use any and all means available. Edgar Allan Poe insisted that he wrote for "effect." He meant *psychological* effect. In photography, we strive for effect within the limits of our medium, which is visual and two-dimensional. For example, I am photographing a group of skyscrapers at fairly close range, using a wide angle lens. But the widest angle lens obtainable (unless I accept the extreme distortion of the 180-degree lens) will take in only a part of the colossal towers. How much shall I attempt to include? Where begin, where leave off? Here the "any and all means" needs explanation. To make up for the lens' optical limitations—the human eye has much greater powers of accommodation—the photographer has to rely on his knowledge of other resources. These include distribution of lights and darks, linear pattern, balance, rhythm, unity, so that psychologically he may reenforce the physical presentation of his subject.

With my example of the skyscrapers, the decision depends on how the subject is interpreted. I may feel that the skyscrapers are beautiful and majestic. Or I may feel that they are ugly, inhuman, illogical, ridiculous, pathological growths which have no place in the planned city. Whatever I think and feel about the skyscrapers, I say through understanding of and application of composition. Vertical lines may seem to topple toward each other, or to fall apart, ready to collapse; they do not create a balanced whole. On the other hand, the photograph may present the skyscrapers in such a manner that verticals sway in a majestic and graceful rhythm expressing unity and order. Even more complex is the problem if the photographer sees the skyscrapers as both beautiful and ugly and seeks to create such a duality in the photograph, by posing opposite tendencies against each other in dynamic composition.

In this instance, the effect is emotional, intellectual, esthetic, factual, social, personal. The subject itself you cannot change; but your opinion of the subject and your emotion about the subject are your own. The idea you seek to convey to others is your own, also. Finally, your expression of that opinion and that idea will be your own, to the extent that you are capable of giving visual reality to subjective factors. You communicate your attitude by organizing a space for the subject within the boundaries of the ground glass. Without question, instinct plays a part in this choice. People with little or no artistic experience will "feel" when a composition is right. What is needed to make the intuitive process conscious and controlled is plenty of practice, a great deal of experimenting. Encourage your innate feeling and allow it to play freely. Enjoy or resent your subject, sympathize with it or disapprove of it. Then try to get your feeling across in the picture itself.

"Composition is an organic and intelligent approach to the problem of saying what you want. It cannot be reduced to a mere mathematical formula," I wrote in my chapter on "The View Camera" in *Graphic Graflex Photography*. "Nevertheless, a few simple rules—applied with a grain of salt—help the beginner. When there is a good reason for breaking a rule, do not hesitate to do so."

I think it is worth while to repeat the rules here:

1. Do not be led astray by rich color in your subject. The photograph must register in values of black and white.

2. The principal subject should not be placed in the mathematical center of the ground glass.

3. Generally, the horizon line should not be in the middle of the ground glass, but above or beneath the middle.

4. Decide if you want your picture to be a horizontal or a vertical. A vertical composition (such as one almost instinctively uses when photographing trees) gives an effect of height, strength, dignity. A horizontal (such as one is induced to use in photographing a view of ocean waves and beach) gives the mood of repose. For practical purposes this decision is made by factors inherent in the subject itself, that is, the dominant direction of the main lines of the picture.

5. Dominant lines may be relieved by secondary lines in opposite directions; this prevents monotony or instability. A mirror-like ocean may be montonous, but a sail slanting from the water serves to break the horizontal tendency and give relief.

6. Not only lines, but also lights and shades need to be balanced. A large shadow should be relieved with a light area or another shadow of lesser intensity. Correct balance of light and shade unifies the photograph.

7. Chief parts of a picture are the principal subject, foreground and background. The subject is the center of interest and as such should attract attention at first glance. Other parts should serve to enhance or reenforce the interest of the main theme.

8. The subject should be the composition's center of unity. There should not be two or more motives of equal interest.

9. If the main subject is far away, introduce elements of interest into the foreground so that it will not be dull. A bush, rocks, a person, a chair, a wagon will serve.

10. If a third or more of the picture is sky, harmony forbids that it should be a blank, white area. Use a light yellow filter and increase exposure by one-half. The sky will then be a light gray instead of a flat white, and white clouds will give relief, as well as enrich the composition.

11. Placing of figures and objects is important. If a person is looking off in one direction, leave more space in front of him than in back. The eyes must have space to look into.

12. To make a figure look tall, place it high in the composition. To make it look small, place it low. Never crowd a stout figure into a small space, unless you deliberately wish to accentuate the impression of weight and size.

The last rule quoted is an excellent proof of the fact that rules about composition are made to be broken. Lisette Model's *The Gambler,* here illustrated, could not conceivably have been placed in an area with ample space about the figure. The sociological significance of the woman, an habitue of Monte Carlo, is underlined by the thrust or push with which she shoves against the borders of the photograph. There is a kind of spatial rapacity about the figure's sheer bulk and mass which is the physical or visual counterpart of the photographer's unspoken but visualized comment. It is interesting to note, also, in connection with Rule 12, a tendency in informal or news portraits to stress this style of composition. The portraits included in the 1941 Press Photographers Association "Photo-Exhibit" show a definite trend in this direction.

That subject matter creates form cannot be repeated too often. Perspective in Renaissance painting was a convention (as spoken and written language is a convention) based on the common consent of its users. The diminishing perspective accepted in that period is no more faithful to nature than the perspective of the 180-degree wide angle lens. Two factors controlled that pictorial convention, the objective and the subjective, classically formal architecture and burgeoning wonder at the world opening out before exploration and discovery. Perspective of photography is controlled by other forces, and should not therefore be expected to bow to a convention based on premises not its own. Even changes in the optical capacity of lenses will serve to alter our conception of what is and what is not good perspective in a photograph. For example, the old print, *Paris Without Signs* (Pl. 9) has a symmetrically placed perspective, due to the fact that the photographer with the materials and equipment available to him at that period (early Third Republic) could not take up any other point of view. Faster lens and faster film today could take the subject from many points

42. THE GAMBLER: MONTE CARLO, 1938 — LISETTE MODEL

Taken with Rolleiflex.

43. EUGÈNE ATGET: PARIS, 1927 — BERENICE ABBOTT

Taken with 9 x 12 cm. view camera; f/4.5 Hermagis lens; glass plate.

of view and still stop the action in the street which the anonymous photographer had to more or less gloss over.

The application of the rules quoted above may be made clearer by discussing some of the photographs reproduced in this book. The question of whether a subject is best rendered in the austere tones of black and white photography, or in the as yet unsatisfactory colors of color photography, is not just a question of personal temperament, as might be argued by some, but is related to the character of the subject itself. For a thousand years, the western world has had picture-making of two kinds, graphic art and painting. Graphic art, of which perhaps photography may be said to be the newest development, is not only a quick, useful expression because it can be multiplied by prints and widely distributed; but it is the correct expression for subjects where form, drawing and tonal values are basic esthetic qualities. It would be absurd to seek to enhance the woodcuts of Dürer with color; they are complete as they are. This is equally true of photography, or perhaps even truer. For the light-sensitiveness of its materials is the perfect mirror of the tones existing in nature, of the textures, surfaces, substances, whose superb rendering in photographs excels the finest renditions of the handcraft arts. *Heymann's Butcher Shop* (Pl. 8) was made because the sheer, shrieking blatancy of the signs called out for recording. The faded, yellowing paper and the red paint are not to my mind particularly paintable; but in black and white (to render the total values of which correctly I used orthochromatic film) the signs shout, they clamor for attention, in visual anarchy. At the same time, the shrewd business sense plastered them solidly over the entire window surface produced, as it were by chance, an esthetic by-product: the whole area simultaneously has homogeneity and variety of texture which gives the photograph interest from the point of view of a picture aside from its human and social interest. It is my feeling, too, that *Night View, Midtown Manhattan* (frontispiece) is a black-and-white subject, though the same view was used as a cover in color for the May, 1941, issue of *Photo Technique*. Essentially, what we see at night is registered by long habit as dark and light, not as color.

Now for Rule 2. William Vandivert's *Michigan Patriarch* (Pl. 11) gives a conventional interpretation of this rule. On the other hand, Hine's *Taking Home Work, East Side,* 1909 (Pl. 45) is proof of how you can break all the rules if you express the reality of your subject. Here it does not matter that a telephone pole is growing out of the woman's head or that she is placed in the mathematical center of the rectangle. There is so much human action, so much character in her powerful stride that she herself controls the picture; formal or traditional composition is a secondary consideration. I might add that this photograph is another example of creative cropping: Hine took the picture as a horizontal with much more space to the right of the figure than to the left. Because of the relative slowness of lens and film at that time (1909) he had to concentrate on the center of interest, the woman, and forget about depth of field, etc.; and the dreary city street of the slum neighborhood is unavoidably out of focus. To focus attention further on his theme, the triumphant, unbowed spirit of the sweatshop worker, Hine trimmed off uninteresting parts of the picture, making the figure larger and more commanding.

Emerson's *A Rushy Shore* (Pl. 24) is a good example of how subject matter creates form, in a creative expression of Rule 3. The composition is almost a stratification of three themes, rushes in the foreground, marsh water in the middle distance, and sky. The picture—a faithful representation of *Life and Landscape on the Norfolk Broads* in 1886, as Emerson called his photographic documentation of this region in what is one of the earliest photographic picture books—is redeemed from a mechanical division of space by the interest of materials, the grassy, growing quality of the rushes, the light reflected on the water, the profile of the buildings against the horizon, even the faint suggestion of clouds in the sky.

Atget's *Country Road* (Pl. 39) shows not only how this rule may be creatively applied, but also another point not listed in the above summary, namely, edge spacing. The points at which important forms or lines break the edges of the photographic area should not be spaced uniformly, like a capital X enclosed in a rectangle, but should impinge on the frame of the picture asymmetrically yet with balance.

The shape of pictures, whether photographs or paintings, is controlled more than we admit by the shape of real objects in nature. Thus, Rule 4 needs to be taken with a grain of salt. To be sure, there will be dominant tendencies in a period—as in a period of fashionable portraiture the vertical will rule, or in an active period of mural painting, the horizontal. However, the twentieth century's *vertikal-tendenz* is plainly the reaction of art to new subject matter, the 1000-foot building. The two photographs reproduced in the next chapter, *Puck* and *Exchange Place* (Pl. 44) could scarcely be done any other way to express their essential mood. On the other hand, Edward Weston's *Dunes at Oceano* (Pl. 48) expresses the emphasis of the photographer—his concern with the frozen perfection of a million tiny particles of sand, shaped into intricate patterns by the drifting action of wind. A vertical shape would bring in a much greater proportion of sky, establish an active relation between earth and sky, and change the meaning of the photograph. As a matter of fact, it may well be that *Michigan Patriarch* (Pl. 11) would have inspired a greater sense of repose and calm in the beholder if it had been composed as a horizontal; certainly it would have been easier to balance the old man's sitting figure with the commanding castiron coal stove in a horizontal space than in vertical.

An exception, however, is *Manhattan Skyline* (Pl. 26). Here the subject requires a horizontal in order to encompass the whole sweep of the panorama. Yet the spirit of the subject is extremely active; indeed, there is a sense of incessant motion about the skyline, the pyramiding of the skyscrapers, the alternations of colors of materials, the way in which the low buildings along the water front are played off against the Cities Service and the Bank of Manhattan Buildings. In *Rockefeller Center* (Pl. 49) the sense of action is the chief emotion to convey, united with the solidity and enduring character of Manhattan Island's basic granite. The vertical shape was the only possible one to use to take in the deep excavation and the steel frame construction rising above. Here the marks of compressed air drills on granite give visual activity to enhance the tension between the two main motives. A further example of how space may intensify the mood of a composition is Hine's home work woman. By cropping, the photographer kept the action concentrated, did not allow the stopped movement of the woman's body to become diffused in space, and so intensified the total psychological effect.

Rule 5 may be illustrated by *Hands of Cocteau* (Pl. 17) in which the strong diagonal chiastic pattern of the crossed hands is relieved by the oval shape of the felt hat on which the hands are folded. The contrasting forms are played against each other to create a kind of visual movement in the composition. In *Exchange Place* (Pl. 44) the upward sweep of the vertical lines would become unendurably monotonous if it were not counteracted by the horizontal motive of sunlight breaking across the dark canyon at the points where cross streets intersect the 35-foot wide Exchange Place.

Walker Evans' *Bethlehem, Pa.* (Pl. 41) is a good example of Rule 6. The complexity of the forms employed and the interplay of tones of varying value might well seem unrelated and chaotic, if the composition had not been brought to a focus by the placing of the large white cross. This solid, simple form creates balance, and at the same time leads the eye back to the smaller cross and so to the smokestacks which are the ultimate objective of the photographer's comment.

Art Class (Pl. 64) illustrates Rule 7. The boy's face is the center of interest; it is happy and at peace, revealing how important the creative outlet of art work is for children. In the foreground is the clay he is modeling; in the background, on a blackboard, a quick sketch of a figure, evidently from another art class. These themes are subsidiary and kept in their place in the picture; yet they serve to accentuate the main theme, by showing the boy's environment at the moment the photograph was taken.

Russell Lee's *Old Woman's Hands* (Pl. 12) is a photograph which breaks all the rules yet observes the important ones. Here is an example of how a part may speak for the whole more eloquently than a thousand wholes could. The skirt and hands are placed in the dead center of the print; the stripes of the skirt's fabric are mathematically centered; even the gnarled knuckles are symmetrical. What is the result? The picture evokes a mood of dead center, also; the emotion is as static as the life of those hands. Here they are, an acute material expression of the human experience of the old woman whose face is not seen. We know more about her than if we had seen her face. The whole history is here of a hard working life—written in texture of skin, drab cloth, dirt ground into human flesh.

With *John Watts* (Pl. 22) the comment is less pathetic, more ironic. What is the center of interest? The statue? The skyscraper's facade? Or the relation between the two, the incongruity of the past which looks up to the present, or of the present which looks down on the past? The bronze may be a monument enduring, but the power and the glory are in the building. Here is a visual parable of our time.

Stock Exchange (Pls. 13 and 14) shows the importance of Rule 9. The first is comparatively empty of human life, and therefore the second version had to be made. The people in the foreground and the use of George Washington's foot are as essential to the composition as the American flag and the sun shining on the portico. Again, Genthe, even in the acute excitement of the *San Francisco Fire* (Pl. 6) managed to get people into the foreground of his picture; and the photograph gains in reality thereby, for costume gives a sense of time.

Rule 10 is illustrated by *Tennessee Barn* (Pl. 38). A filter brought out the clouds, so that the variation of white and light gray in the sky offered a counterweight to the rich texture of the stone barn.

Hine's *Orphan* (Pl. 40) is a marvellous demonstration of how to break all the rules. How magnificently the figure of the child is placed. The perspective is distorted; yet this distortion is emotionally expressive, for it brings everything in the picture to focus on the child. The visual compulsion exercised by this distorted perspective is such that the eyes rush to the little orphan. Her situation in life is brought inescapably to the attention. A legitimate pathos is transmuted into a more profound emotion, the tragedy of disinherited children. The girl's dirty clothes and pudgy feet, the latter perhaps a symptom of malnutrition, are the accents of her loneliness. Another Hine photograph, *This Is Such A Friendly Town* (Pl. 68), has a similarly poignant emotional appeal, which is certainly due in part to the fact that Hine intuitively found an eloquent compositional language. Again, perspective leads the eye to the figure. The old woman is bowed down as she sits on the hard piece of sewer pipe; the weight of her position seems so great that one doubts if she could ever be lifted up. Even a detail like the cigar butt is expressive; it was tossed away without thought, as the friendless woman was. Try cutting off some of the space to the left of the figure, and see how differently it will affect you. Then the intelligent application of composition will be better understood.

Atget's *Cabriolet* (Pl. 23) combines placing and edging spacing with a further element. The horse has been cut ruthlessly in two, like a Munchausen tale. But this is not important. Atget wanted to compel people to see the vehicle itself, a type even in his time beginning to go out of use. Its aura of time past no doubt fascinated him, and probably he loved the cabriolet for itself, shape and all. To make the cabriolet as large as possible and to use all of his rectangle, he had to employ a vertical and slash the horse in two. Here again, content controlled composition (form).

In regard to Rule 12, Hine's *Orphan* (Pl. 40) may be referred to once more, to illustrate the importance of placing a figure low in the composition to accentuate its smallness. The Model *The Gambler,* as said before, represents the crowding of a figure into an area to emphasize its largeness. The *Portrait of Orozco* (Pl. 33) makes use of the same device, but with a somewhat different emotional slant; the large head is placed with little space around it to suggest the monumentality of the modeling of the Mexican mural painter's face, but also the monumentality of his painting gift and of his character.

The above analyses illustrate how photographers find ways to say what they want to say. Actually, a sense of composition is developed more and more as you photograph. When your pictures do not satisfy you, analyze them severely for the reason. In the majority of cases, failure is due to not composing your subject correctly. Prints are often easier to analyze, because of their small size, than the big life size subject in nature. It is, therefore, profitable, as well as a good method of training the eye, to retake the picture, having the first photograph beside you and seeing directly how you can balance it better the second time and make it say more effectively what you mean. Few mediums train the eye as acutely as photography, where experience accumulates a store of visual memories and awareness.

44*a*. PUCK BERENICE ABBOTT
Taken with 8 x 10 Century Universal view camera; single element of 59 cm. convertible Zeiss Protar lens. A subject in which cropping of negative is necessary.

44*b*. EXCHANGE PLACE BERENICE ABBOTT
Taken with 8 x 10 Century Universal view camera; 7 inch Goerz Dagor lens. Another subject in which cropping is necessary.

45. TAKING HOME WORK: EAST SIDE, 1909 LEWIS W. HINE

Enlarged from part of a 5 x 7 negative to enhance effectiveness of content, as explained in the text.

Courtesy of Corydon Hine

46. A GOOD EXAMPLE OF ADVERTISING ART LEO AARONS

Projection control produced this amusing ad for Arrow Shirts. The montage was awarded a certificate of distinctive merit at the 20th annual Art Directors Exhibition this year.

Courtesy of Cluett, Peabody Co.

47. TENANCINGO, MEXICO, 1933 — Paul Strand

Taken with 5 x 7 Home Portrait Graflex, using prism; 1/5 second; f/30.
Masked to same proportions as 8 x 10. Contact print.

16. Enlarging

TODAY the battle which used to rage around the question, "Shall I enlarge my photographs?" does not seem very immediate. No doubt, there survives a handful of perfectionists, the purest of the pure, the straightest of the straight, who still raise their eyebrows at the thought of an enlargement. But in these times when photographers are seeking to make their work have wide human appeal through means of photomurals, photomontage, photographic picture books, magazine reproductions, photojournalism, etc., it seems rather unimportant to debate the issue. The fact is that the vast majority of photographers, for one reason or another, make enlargements or have them made. In the conventional art world of museums, galleries and exhibitions, the enlargement is a more sensible way of presenting photographs than sticking up postage stamp sized prints on the wall, as if photography were the rarest and most precious of portfolio mediums.

From the point of view of content and also of esthetic effect, there are definite advantages in enlarging, not to say that you are practically forced to enlarge films under 5 x 7. In small prints, details are so tiny in scale that the eye fails to take them in or see their importance. Enlarged, the details come to life. A further advantage is that when you enlarge, only a part of the negative need be used, and undesirable and unimportant sections can be excluded. You can thus try out different effects, improve and balance your composition, intensify the emphasis you sought.

This is written with full understanding that in the last analysis the creative photographer controls his picture when he takes it—of course within the framework of existing conditions. Because I believe in photography as a medium controlled by human intelligence and skill, I have advocated that you work with ground glass cameras in which you really are able to see your picture as you take it. However, there are many cases in which you cannot completely see the picture or completely control external facts. If you need to work with a miniature camera to stop action under bad light, you can scarcely compose your picture as meticulously as you do with a ground glass camera. Or it may be that your subject is of a nature which does not fit into the rather hackneyed proportions of the 4 x 5 or 8 x 10 rectangle. Definitely you need to bring your picture to life by a final act of selection, or editorial revision as it were, in enlarging. In fact, the conventional format of film in a way imposes a slavery on the eye which perhaps can only be resisted by "cropping."

In both *Exchange Place* and *Puck,* here illustrated, I had the problem of finding a shape suitable to the subject. These two subjects, quite different in meaning and emotional impact, exemplify the twentieth century *vertikal-tendenz* mentioned in the chapter on composition. Only the modern, unplanned American city can offer these deep architectural vistas as a theme. The narrowness of the street, Exchange Place, the overpowering fashion in which the tall buildings crowd in from either side, the occasional interruptions of patches of bright sunlight, the crowds hurrying antlike about, express a concentration of life and human activity. In taking the photograph, I had naturally to take in the fronts of the two buildings which flank the opening of Exchange Place from Broadway. However, those facades were meaningless in relation to the idea I wished to present. So the print had to be trimmed to eliminate the irrelevant. This left me with a contact print 9½ inches high and 2¼ inches wide. For exhibition purposes or to put on the wall of a room, this size was ridiculous. Hence, the necessity for enlarging. So, too, with *Puck.* Here is a sort of antiquity or curiosity of New York. The building on which it is fastened is not the significant thing in the picture, but the figure. Again, cropping was an essential step in making the photograph.

An enlargement is simply a print larger than the negative from which it is made. The principle of enlarging is similar to that of motion picture projection, that is, light travels through the negative and is focused on the printing paper by means of a lens. Enlarging is often spoken of as "projection printing" and the paper (bromide, described in Chapter 12) as "projection paper." Enlargers, which make possible this projection, may be either vertical or horizontal. They vary considerably in cost, size and type. *Photographic Buyers Handbook* gives a good analysis of available equipment.

There are too many enlargers on the market to make choice simple. However, there are specifications, which are imperative, whether the enlarger costs little or much and without which it is useless for all practical purposes. These may be summed up as follows:

1. The enlarger must be rigid so that vibrations will not shake it.

2. The lens board must be absolutely parallel to the negative carrier and to the easel or table (as with the vertical models) or the wall (as with the horizontal) which holds the printing paper.

3. Some enlargers have lenses with no diaphragm. But I strongly urge only buying an enlarger whose lens has a diaphragm. Exposures of less than 10 seconds are not advisable when making enlargements. If the negative should be especially thin, using the diaphragm at a smaller opening enables you to give the minimum length of exposure, namely 10 seconds, without overexposing the print. Likewise when more time is required for necessary dodging, the diaphragm can be closed down. This structural feature is essential for flexibility of operation and of control. If you make use of a tilting easel or find it necessary to tip the paper, the lens must have a diaphragm to focus the over-all image. Tilting in such cases is done to straighten converging lines or to distort deliberately for effect. A further usefulness of the diaphragm is for closing down to give time for "spot" printing, with or without montage.

4. If you enlarge from negatives of different size, it is necessary to use different lenses, hence the need for easily interchangeable lens boards. Anastigmatic lenses with good flatness of field should be used. Even these are not perfect, and in most cases for films larger than miniature, openings of no more than f/5.6 or f/6.8 should be employed. A valuable aid to test the best opening for your lens is to use a focusing film (like the Utilo, which costs from 25 to 65 cents) to facilitate the focusing of sharp point images to the corners of the enlargement.

5. The light source used in enlargers ranges from mercury vapor tubes and carbon arcs to electric bulbs, the latter being most common. The stronger the light the better, because time is saved in exposing prints and also because slower and better quality paper may be used. A strong light, however, requires definite safeguards. The lamp house must be well ventilated to

avoid overheating film and lens; yet the light must not leak during exposure. Moreover, the light must produce complete evenness of illumination. Light in enlargers is either diffused or condensed. It is diffused by the use of opal glass diffusers so that the transmitted illumination is even and free from filament reflections. Contrasted with diffusers are condensers, like huge lenses, which condense and distribute the light rays evenly. Condensers tend to make the light intense and the image brilliant. For miniature film and small film generally, condenser enlargers are desirable and universally used.

Before working with your enlarger, test the lighting for even illumination, which is essential, otherwise your enlargements will be of uneven blackness and whiteness, the uneven lighting producing prints of uneven density. The test is simple. Turn on the light in the enlarger and project it on the easel or wall. The lens' diaphragm should be wide open. Focus the light by making the outline of the negative carrier sharp. If the light is not even or if illumination falls off at any side or corner, the light source should be adjusted, the lens should be checked for the fault, or the construction of the enlarger should be gone over.

The negative carrier is another essential structure of the enlarger. For negatives larger than 35 mm., the film is usually placed between two pieces of glass to keep it flat. The sensitive side must face the lens and easel. If the negative is smaller than the smallest size negative carrier your enlarger takes, a blackmask should be placed around it between the pieces of glass, so that stray light will not reflect when it strikes the easel. Care should be taken, generally, that stray light reflected from a light colored wall or other light objects does not strike the printing paper on the easel.

Except for the lamp house, the enlarger is a great deal like a camera, with bellows and lens. The bellows is flexible to focus the lens. In fact, some simple enlargers are built to use with your own camera (the Kodak type as a rule,) using the camera's lens for enlarging. As with your camera, know your enlarger! It has a number of adjustments for you to turn, slide up or down or sidewise, to make your composition on the easel as you wish. A great deal of creative composing may take place on the easel of your enlarger. Learn to make use of its possibilities.

Negatives intended for enlarging must be more critically sharp than those for contact printing. *This point first and foremost.* They must also be *cleaner* than any other negatives; therefore, they must be free from scratches, dirt, fingermarks, dust. If they are not, all these will be enlarged proportionally and cause endless retouching and spotting on the finished print. The pieces of glass which hold the film in the enlarger must likewise be clean and flawless.

Negatives for enlarging should never be underexposed; a negative fully exposed with adequate shadow detail is best. The negative should be fairly thin. At this point, I must mention the fact that the degree of contrast to which it is desirable to develop your negative depends somewhat on the type of enlarger you own. A condenser enlarger, all other things being equal, gives a more contrasty print than an enlarger with diffused light. Therefore, with a condenser enlarger, you will do well to develop your film a minute or two less (experience will tell you precisely how much less) than you would for a diffuser type enlarger.

Finally, and no less important, negatives to be enlarged should never be overdense. When a negative is too dense, it is almost impossible to see detail clearly enough to focus or to judge the composition. Moreover, there is danger of overheating the enlarger, equally bad for negative and lens. Furthermore, dense negatives due to overdevelopment are grainier, which is even less desirable in enlarging than in contact printing.

Contact prints are made with chloride paper in contact with the negative, light being transmitted through the film. Enlargements are made by transmitting light from the lamp house through the negative to the projection paper. The kind of paper used for contact prints is out of the question for projection prints because exposure would take hours instead of minutes. Bromide paper is made, therefore, especially to answer this problem. If your enlarger is an exceptionally fast one, chlorobromide paper (which is slower than bromide) can be used; it offers some fine quality papers. The source of light being equal, a condenser enlarger is faster than a diffuser enlarger.

Choice of surface and color of paper depends on personal taste. In my opinion, white or natural white is most beautiful, and a paper which has a slight "tooth" or roughness is good for enlarging. Papers like Eastman *Proof Bromide, P.M.C. 11,* Agfa *Brovira Royal,* and some types of Defender *Velour Black,* are standard.

Darkroom equipment for enlarging is the same as for contact printing unless your trays are too small to hold large sized prints. Use the developer recommended by the paper's manufacturer. In most cases, Eastman D72 is satisfactory if you buy your developer already prepared. However, instead of diluting the stock solution one part developer to two parts water as in contact printing, for bromide paper dilute one part stock solution to four parts water. For developing enlargements, keep the developer at 70 degrees. Use the safelight specified for the paper you choose.

The steps in enlarging may be summarized as follows:

1. Remove negative carrier and clean glass. Dust negative with brush and place face down in the carrier.

2. Move the enlarger up and down (or backwards and forwards) to get the projected image the approximate size you wish.

3. Focus the image by moving the lens closer to or farther away from the easel or wall. If the image is not then the proper size, again move the enlarger up and down slightly and focus again. With an auto focus enlarger, no focusing is necessary.

4. During the above step, carefully arrange your composition. If you wish, you can enlarge only a section of the negative. A slight turn, a little more or a little less cropping, may vastly improve the effect.

5. Select the proper grade of contrast to suit the negative, remembering that if the negative is hard or contrasty to use softer paper, and vice versa.

6. Tear a sheet of paper into test strips, and place a strip on the easel over the most important part of the image.

7. Make tests of, say, 10, 15 and 20 seconds. The correct exposure may seem to be about 15 seconds. Then make exposures of 13 and 17 seconds, to narrow down exposure time. This estimated time will prove a good guide for the exposure of the first full sheet of paper. Only the whole print can determine precise exposure.

8. Develop the test strips for the time indicated in instructions, usually a minimum of 1½ minutes. Projection papers develop more slowly than contact papers. The 1½ minutes is much more flexible, however, than the 45 seconds specified for contact prints. To vary the result, sometimes expose less; but in most cases, a full two or even three minute development gives superior quality. As a general rule, an exposure which develops the

print fully in two minutes is best. For the first minute, protect your print by keeping it face down in the developer, rocking the tray gently. However, only through familiarity with a given paper can you judge the best peak of development time. Longer exposure and shorter development tend to flatten the print, while shorter exposure and longer development make the print more contrasty.

9. Rinse the print in an "acid short stop bath" (1½ ounces of 28 per cent acetic acid to 32 ounces of water), fix, wash and dry in the same manner as for contact prints.

Local Dodging of Prints

A great advantage of enlarging over contact printing, is the ease it offers for dodging. The word means just that, dodging the light from parts of the print. If conditions for taking photographs were always ideal, if all negatives were 100 per cent perfect, if every photographer could own first-class equipment, the need for such corrections as dodging would disappear. However, to produce a perfect negative even with all the knowledge and skill in the world is not always possible. There may be external factors which result in a negative of unequal density. In contact printing, there are ways of remedying such a condition. Also, for both contact printing and enlarging, retouching the negative with new coccine (as explained in Chapter 18) will help correct unavoidable inadequacies in the negative. However, dodging is a somewhat more flexible and plastic way of achieving the same end. It permits a certain amount of legitimate modeling or fading of the edges of one area into the adjacent area.

In dodging, you intercept light from the lamp house, holding it back from thin areas of the negative, which would otherwise print too dark. You can make your own dodger, if you wish, attaching a piece of heavy cardboard or even a wad of cotton to a stiff wire handle; or there are any number of readymade gadgets on the market for the purpose, some being very fancy little items of celluloid, in various shapes and colors. The handle should be at least a foot long so that the shadow of the hand will not fall on the print. The dodger is held at some distance from the easel, to prevent its casting shadows with sharply defined edges. It must never be held still but must be gently and evenly moved back and forth so that no line of demarcation or too light area appears in the print. Dodging is almost like using a brush and painting with light. Perhaps there is a dense corner or edge to the negative, giving a faded and weak corner to the print. Hold a cardboard between the light and the paper, and keep in in motion, to hold back light from the entire print *except* the edge or corner. Count the additional length of time for this purpose, as several trials may be necessary.

48. DUNES AT OCEANO, CALIFORNIA, 1936 — Edward Weston

Taken with 8 x 10 view camera.

49. ROCKEFELLER CENTER, 1932 BERENICE ABBOTT

Taken with 8 x 10 Century Universal view camera; 9½ inch Goerz Dagor; 1/5 second; f/22.

50. MOTHER BIRD FEEDING HER YOUNG — Eliot Porter

4 x 5 view camera.

Courtesy of An American Place

51*a*. TOM GAY DILLON
Taken with 4 x 5 Speed Graphic; Zeiss Tessar 5¼ inch lens; f/9; medium yellow filter; Defender XF Panchromatic cut film; on late August afternoon. Contact print from original negative, uncropped and unretouched.

51*b*. TOM GAY DILLON
Coccine was used to bring out the words "Button Mill" and to lighten the hair. The enlargement was cropped to improve composition.

17. The Art of Printing

AT EVERY step in photography we pause and say "*This* step is vital. If *this* link breaks, the whole chain is broken. Is there, indeed, one phase of greater importance than another? Can we say that making the correct exposure is more important than developing the film properly? Or that either of these steps is more vital than printing? When we try to weigh questions like these, we are forced back on the paradox of photography—its complex and interlocking character.

However, just to cut the Gordian knot for once, let's take a stand and make a forthright assertion flatfootedly. If every step has been meticulously and correctly carried out and if printing is badly done, then the whole process is defeated. Not until the photograph can greet the world as an accomplished fact, a picture in black and white, or in color, can it be said in any real sense to exist. The vision you had when you clicked the shutter is meaningless unless it achieves visualization. What you dream is your private, subjective fantasy. Only the reality of the finished print, as beautiful and convincing as your imagined picture, can speak to the hundreds, thousands, millions, who never knew what you saw with your inner vision.

So—printing is crucial. By the print, whether contact or enlargement, the aims of the photographer must be vindicated. Here is the photograph, rich, glowing, luminous, brilliant, capable of arousing emotion, lovely in its own physical self. And how did it get that way? Because the photographer had a sense of the medium, because he had a flair for printing, because by patient exercise he mastered the discipline of his technique.

A synthesis of experience is achieved at the time the print emerges from the developer, just as coordination of skills is needed when you click the shutter. A number of perceptions are involved and coordinated in that final click when your fate is sealed; for, before that click, you have selected your subject, chosen your point of view and angle, determined the lighting effect wanted, gauged perspective, and calculated exposure, so that everything is set for the final peak of instantaneous action and interest. If haste is necessary, you have accumulated enough experience so as to be able quickly to coordinate all these decisions and operations. Consequently, the role of photographer is tense, all nerves focused toward this one precise moment. Concentrating the faculties on the crucial moment requires keen alertness and consciousness and consumes more nervous energy than work where the effort is spread out over hours instead of minutes.

In printing, a like intensity prevails. Precise exposure in seconds and precise development and manipulation, all consciously and quickly controlled, call for a similar alertness and awareness on the part of the photographer. Hence the slogan; for good printing, experience! Better make many prints from one negative to get one good print, than ten bad prints from ten negatives, good or bad. Prints which are made with lukewarm interest or "let the print take care of itself" mood are never good prints. In most cases, you have to sweat to get a good print.

A great many prints made in the robot fashion of letting mechanically timed exposure and development do the work appear overbright, hence unreal. No doubt, you have seen prints of interiors where everything in the room sparkled like an advertisement. What is wanted is a print with the depth and atmosphere of an inside room which is never as bright as if the room were laid out like a stage setting on a sunlit plain. The error comes from the attitude that print-making is purely mechanical. Alas, too many prints look just that way: they look too *photographic!* They lack spirit, depth, atmosphere, control. I believe that this unreal untendency can be overcome if you make a visual transition from the print back to the scene photographed and vice versa. For, when you took the picture, you certainly tried to visualize the scene as a photographic print and to decide what characteristics and qualities you wanted to stress or, better, *enhance* in the print. You must have wanted, most of all, to recreate visually in your photograph the same atmosphere, the same light quality, the same sensory, emotional effect you experienced when you were prompted to take the picture. Above all, when taking a photograph, try to see light as it will register in the print.

The idea which led you to make a certain shot falls short if you cannot convey to others what you yourself felt. The print is not expressive unless the entire processing is tied up step by step with the taking, making and printing of your picture. All negatives are not perfect. Compromises must too often be made with exposure so that in the final analysis prints must be manipulated, juggled, analysed critically. The factor most to be considered in making a good print is correct balance of contrast. The print is made for effect more than for mechanical representation; it should, therefore, be studied for what to subdue, what to emphasize.

If all our negatives were of normal contrast, printing would be a simple matter. Unfortunately, conditions of photography do not allow even the most expert to turn out one hundred per cent of perfect negatives. The goal toward which to work is a normal negative; by keeping exposure records and by analysing results, you may hope to approach this goal. In the meanwhile you have to work with what you have: negatives inadequately exposed because conditions did not permit fuller exposure, contrasty negatives because they were overdeveloped, thin negatives because they were underexposed or overdeveloped, dense negatives because they were overexposed or underdeveloped or both, flat negatives because the lighting was flat or they were underdeveloped. You can't throw out all these pictures because they aren't perfect. You want to salvage what you can from them, learn what you can. The first step is to analyse the differences so that at the beginning you can tell what type of negative you have. The ultimate purpose of classifying negatives is to develop your skill in selecting the right grade of contrast of paper for a given negative.

What does this mean? You know that paper comes in different colors, surfaces and textures. These are material differences. However, paper also comes in different contrasts, which are chemical differences. Thus, the composition of a paper's emulsion is varied, in order to produce different kinds of prints. Prints, like negatives, may be normal, contrasty, flat, dense, etc. To compensate for unavoidable deficiencies or failures of negatives, you use a paper of opposite character. Contrast is the pivot around which quality of prints revolves. It is a term frequently heard and frequently misused. The difference between the negative's lightest and darkest parts measures contrast, because this spread determines the range between a photograph's blacks and whites. If a negative lacks contrast, it is called flat. What is needed in printing is compensation for this characteristic. If the flat, thin negative is printed on a hard or extra hard paper, a satisfactory print may in most cases be produced. Contrariwise, if a hard or contrasty negative is printed on a soft paper, a good print should result, providing your exposure, development and manipulations are correct.

When you start out to make a good print, there are several mechanical steps to take care of first. The developer should be fresh, properly mixed and at the correct temperature. Next, the proper grade of paper should be selected for your negative. Unless your work is developed to a point where you can print on one grade of paper, you must have on hand a selection of grades of paper. The proper grade cannot always be chosen by examining the film. Perhaps a few tests or prints must be made first. Once the correct grade is ascertained, exposure must be determined by making several tests. Now you have an approximate print to judge.

Your best judgment presupposes that you know what you wish to emphasize or to subdue and the over-all effect you want to create. Do you want some details minimized? Let that area print darker or manipulate the print by "spot" printing, that is, by letting a spot of light pass through a hole in a cardboard to give more light to one area, while holding back light from other areas. If you need more detail in parts and cannot get it from a straight print because the negative is not perfectly balanced, dodging (as described in the last chapter) may be resorted to. If the area to be held back is too precise for dodging and if the shadow parts of the negative are thin but have detail, new coccine can be used on that part of the negative which is to appear lighter in the final print. New coccine (which is a red dye, described more fully in the next chapter) is a good medium for holding back light from local areas, usually shadow parts which the latitude of present-day papers fail to deal with.

To bring out stubborn high lights, friction can be used, rubbing that part of the print with the fingers, the warmth and touch of which hasten development of that area. Some photographers use a wad of cotton dipped in a concentrated solution of developer and rub areas meant to be brought out. Conversely, you can manipulate the print in this manner to darken areas which you wish subdued. Even a warm breath gently blown on a part of the print will hasten development.

For nearly all types of printing paper of normal contrast, additional bromide is needed in the developer. Two or three drops of saturated solution of potassium bromide peps up the print by making the whites whiter. With a little practice, you will recognize when and if the additional bromide is sufficient.

To make good prints, it is important to be thoroughly familiar with the paper you use. Some papers dry down darker and need to be taken from the developer sooner than appearances warrant. Other papers reach a better over-all tone by longer than prescribed development time, while still others reach their best development at the median time. *Azo,* for instance, develops nearly always to its best peak in 45 seconds, this for contact prints, of course. Many enlarging papers develop best from 1½ to 2 minutes; but there are quite a few exceptions, some projection papers giving the best result with a 3-minute development.

A factor which differs from merely holding back or lightening some areas while darkening others has to do with the controlled and exact amount of contrast. Assuming that the correct grade of paper has been chosen, there are various means other than straight development which will lessen or increase the degree of contrast in the print. These are outlined in the following table:

TO MAKE PRINTS MORE CONTRASTY	TO MAKE PRINTS SOFTER
Use more concentrated developer	Dilute developer with more water than formula calls for
Give shorter exposure, longer development	Give longer exposure, shorter development
Overdevelop and later reduce with Farmer's reducer	Soak print in water after exposing and before placing in developer
Use additional hydroquinone, carbonate or bromide	Use more metol, less hydroquinone

Regarding Point 4, it is not advisable to tamper with formulas unless you understand the principles of photographic chemistry and are willing to put in considerable time experimenting and making test prints for comparison.

Another method which is a favorite for controlling the effect of prints is two tray development, in which the print is alternated between two trays containing two types of developer. Two developers used for this method are Agfa 120 and Agfa 130. Agfa 120 is a soft developer; and when the print is first placed in it, shadow detail and soft tones appear. Then when there is enough shadow detail, the print is placed in Agfa 130, which gives the print brilliance. This developer contains glycin and does not fog the print easily so that a longer development is possible. Also, fine blacks are produced. The print can be manipulated between these two developers for the desired effect.

Other factors which produce contrast but which cannot be manipulated are listed in the following table:

FACTORS PRODUCING CONTRASTY PRINTS	FACTORS PRODUCING SOFT PRINTS
Orthochromatic film	Panchromatic film
Slow film, slow paper	Fast film, fast bromide paper
Condenser enlarger	Diffuser enlarger
Naturally contrasty subjects, such as portraits, sun and shadow subjects, and interiors	Distance scenes and landscapes; flat lighting

Finally, to go back a step, there is an experiment which will help you solve many of your printing problems. The experiment integrates the entire technical process and leads to good prints without manipulation, by enabling you to make properly balanced negatives. It is advisable to carry out the experiment twice, once for outdoor work and once for indoor work with artificial light.

Experiment

A. Select a subject with lighting conditions which will remain constant throughout the test. If outdoors, use light which will not play hide-

and-seek with a cloud, but which is unobscured. Be sure that there are important shadows with desired detail in the chosen subject. Use your exposure film rating and judge exposure according to formula. Place your camera on the tripod, and now give the first exposure your *calculated* time. Then, in quick succession and with your subject and shadows the same, give five more exposures, varying the time of each; say, if the calculated time calls for 1/10 second, give in all six exposures at the same aperture, at 1 second, 1/2, 1/5, 1/10, 1/25 and 1/50 second. Have your developer ready at the correct temperature, and develop the films immediately for the minimum time of development. If development time is said to be 10 to 15 minutes, develop for 10 minutes. Judge the negatives only for shadow detail and general exposure density. If you think that the negative which had 1/10 second exposure is most nearly correct, you have good reason to be satisfied with your meter or calculator *plus* your own interpretation of how the reading should be taken. If, however, the best negative for adequate shadow detail is the one which had ½ second exposure, adjust your calculations with exposure meter accordingly, allowing a factor of five for error in film ratings, as the ½ second exposure is five times the estimated 1/10 second.

B. Now make ten exposures of the same subject, giving them all the same time under the same conditions, i.e., exposures at ½ second. Then develop these films for different lengths of time, varying time by one minute. Be sure to have the developer the correct temperature throughout the test. With a stated development time of 10 to 15 minutes, develop the ten exposurs 7, 8, 9, 10, 11, 12, 13, 14, 15 and 16 minutes. Then compare results. The best way to tell if a negative is properly developed is to judge by the print, and, if your negatives are to be enlarged, this means the enlargement. When the films are dry, make the best possible print on *normal* paper from all ten negatives. The film which gives the best print denotes the best developing time for you with your particular type of equipment, enlarger, etc. If you have a condenser enlarger, it is possible that you should develop your films a minute or two less than a person with a diffuser enlarger who would need to develop his film longer for best results with normal paper.

18. Finishing the Photograph

FINISHING the print is the photographer's last action before it can go out into the world—whether the world of the close family circle, the salon or the editor's desk. If the photographer has mastered his technic in order to be able to communicate what he has to say, then the presentation of his idea is the last proof he can give of his sincerity; for bad presentation can wreck a good photograph. The most progressive contemporary photographers have put behind them "art for art's sake." With the new vanguard, the conception of technic for technic's sake is no longer valid. On the contrary, the usefulness of superb technic and excellent equipment is now believed to be due to the fact that they widen the range of communication of photography. The more the photographer can learn about his medium the more he can say. Thereafter, the impact of what he says is determined by the richness of his experience, by how he sees and feels, by how profoundly and seriously he thinks about what he has seen and felt.

If it is worth while to go to a great amount of labor to practice photography in this spirit, it follows logically that the photographer should not let his idea fail of comprehension due to slipshod presentation. All the steps which must be carried out between the time the print leaves the hypo and is hung on the wall involve careful workmanship. Drying, straightening, trimming, cropping, mounting, are essential parts of this last phase in making a photograph.

Drying Prints

Once the prints are dry, they need to be straightened. This is no problem in a photofinishing plant where prints are placed wet and squeegeed on large ferrotype tins which revolve around a heater and are quickly dried flat. Where space permits, the amateur can dry prints on racks of clean muslin stretched on wooden frames, and the curl in the prints will be slight. However, most amateurs dry prints by hanging them to dry, and curl is therefore something to deal with. It is advisable to place clips at the bottom of prints as well as at the top. They can be hung up, two together, back to back, to save space and labor. Placing the prints between blotters is not to my mind a good drying method. If they are placed between blotters while still too wet, there is a danger that the face of the print will stick to the blotter. There is also the problem of replacing the blotters frequently enough to be sure that they are absolutely clean.

Glossy prints can be dried on ferrotype tins and, when dry, fall off flat, with a high gloss. There are disadvantages, however, to this method. Beside the additional cost of the tins, great care must be taken to keep them free from scratches and absolutely clean; and frequent polishing with ferrotype polish is necessary to keep the surface perfectly smooth. In ferrotyping, prints are placed wet, face down, on the tins, and clean blotters are placed on top; then the whole is rolled firmly with a hand squeegee. If you use a number of tins, they should be wrapped separately in tissue paper when not in use or placed in a rack with shelves for each tin. If the ferrotype tins are not clean and free from scratches, the prints will dry with some spots dull, some glossy, or they may stick to the tin and not come off, or dry in uneven rings or ridges.

Straightening

Prints curl more in winter than in summer and are more brittle, requiring greater care in handling, not to crack the emulsion. If they curl too much, try steaming them by holding the face of the print toward steam from a boiling kettle and moving it about slowly. Steam will remove the worst curl so that you can flatten the print more by other means. This is usually done by moistening a wad of cotton with water or with half wood alcohol and half water and dampening the back of the prints, which must not be made too wet. Then stack them together and place them under a flat weight, a dry mounting press being ideal. The backs can also be dampened with a solution of 1 part of glycerin to 3 parts of water. If the print has not curled too much and if the emulsion is not too brittle, it can be straightened by pulling it firmly over a smooth table edge. Holding the print down against the table edge with one hand, pull with the other alternately toward the print's four corners, the face of the print being up. To dry prints with less curl, some photographers bathe them after their final washing in a bath composed of 2 ounces glycerin to 32 ounces water, and let them remain in this solution not less than five minutes without further washing before hanging up. In any case, prints must be reasonably flat to spot and absolutely flat to mount.

Retouching

Retouching on a big scale is rarely done by amateurs or even by professionals; for it requires experience and time and is a highly specialized job. However, simple retouching, such as spotting, can be done by every photographer who will take the time to learn how and, indeed, is often unavoidable. Understanding of the method and a little patient practice on old prints will do the trick. If you wish to spend your life on negatives and prints, gilding the lily as it were, a helpful reference is "*The Art of Retouching and Improving Negatives and Prints,* for which see the bibliography. Luckily, most photographers are so eager to take pictures that they are saved from the worst excesses to which retouching, practiced in a mechanical spirit, can lead. Taft in *Photography and the American Scene* has some interesting historical material dealing with the dawn of retouching as a photographic trade. However, for our purposes, neither trade nor history is imperative; a few simple instructions will do.

Most white spots on prints are caused by dust in the enlarger or the printer; and great care must be taken to prevent stray particles of foreign matter of any sort settling on the film while printing. Likewise, the glass holding the film in the enlarger and all parts of the printer should be kept spotless. Black spots on prints are due to dust in the camera or film holders and cause "pinholes" or tiny transparent holes in the negative, which print black. It is practically impossible to retouch on small negatives; but in the case of larger negatives which have pinholes, spotting is best done on the film. For the most part, all kinds of spots are caused by carelessness, hence one of the reasons for my repeated pleas for extreme cleanliness and neatness in the darkroom.

52. CHILD IN SURF — ANSEL ADAMS

Kodak Ektra; 50 cm. f/1.9 Ektar; 1/500 second; f/5.6; Panatomic film; Eastman DK20 developer.

Courtesy of Chudwick Seaside School, Rolling Hills, California

53. ARTIST AT WORK — Max Yavno

Taken with 4 x 5 Linhof; 8¼ Dagor lens; 2 seconds; f/22; daylight; Isopan film; Eastman D76; enlargement on Vitava Projection F2; developed in D72. An example of informal portraiture in intimate surroundings.

It is desirable to practice spotting prints before you attempt spotting negatives. The following materials and tools are needed: a small tube of ivory black water color; a medium sized sable brush with a fine point for spotting; Eagle Turquoise lead holder with electronic graphite HB leads; a razor blade; fine emery paper; retouching fluid; small paper stumps from an art store; new coccine; a small block or jar of opaque.

Daylight is best for retouching prints. But if you have to use artificial light, let it be indirect. All light should come over the left shoulder, not to cast a shadow on the print. Place a small amount of the spotting color on a dish and get the wet brush full of color, working out excess moisture on a sheet of paper and at the same time bringing the brush to a fine point and matching the tone of the color to the tone of the print so that the spot disappears. If the brush is too wet, a shiny spot will remain on the print, so that it is better to have the brush almost dry and gently build up the spot. Spotting white spots on prints is actually a dotting process where the white spots or white lines are dotted out or removed with tiny little strokes. Larger spots should be built up little by little. If a mistake is made or the spotting color too dark, wipe it off with moist cotton and begin over. Although in spotting attention is directed mainly toward repairing the damage caused by lint or dust spots, you can also use the spotting technic to get rid of objectionable small parts of a print, such as undesirable high lights or distracting forms.

Black spots on the print are "etched" out. This amounts to shaving the print emulsion very gently and delicately. A sharp razor blade is suitable, although there are special tools for the purpose. The corner of the blade is stroked lightly back and forth over the spot or area, care being observed not to scratch or dig into the emulsion.

Retouching on the negative is more delicate and needs more practice. Etching on the film is not advisable since only skilled retouchers do the job well. However, since etching is much less desirable even on a print than on a negative, it is better to solve the dilemma by filling in the pinhole on the negative which produces the black spot on the print. Then a white spot will appear on the print instead of a black one. To do this, the brush is filled with moist opaque, which is then dotted into the pinhole on the negative.

Any other retouching on the negative is usually done with pencil.

Since pencil does not adhere to the emulsion, retouching fluid is first applied. With the tip of the cork, place a dab of fluid on several parts of the film and rub the entire surface evenly and firmly with a circular motion, using a good sized wad of clean cotton and spreading the fluid uniformly and drily. Care must be exercised not to mark the negative with fingermarks or dust, since the surface is tacky from the fluid. The negative is then placed on the retouching stand; or in a pinch, your printer may be used. A magnifying glass may help you to see more clearly. Long leads in the pencil holder are worked up to a very fine point with emery paper. The point should be two or three inches long, so that the lightest touch can be made when working on the negative. Holding the pencil lightly, brush the side of the lead across the surface to be retouched, moving the lead with a circular motion, as if you were superimposing many little 6s, 8s and 9s with a rotary stroke, gradually building up the area. On larger areas, the paper stump is used to smooth out the pencil.

Work of this kind is often done on portraits when wrinkles, blemishes, deep shadows from artificial light, stray wisps of hair, moles, whiskers, etc., need to be subdued or eliminated. Since glossy paper has a shiny surface, penciling is done in the same manner as on a negative, giving the print a slightly tacky surface with retouching fluid. As most glossy prints are designed for reproduction, this is not serious, as it would be if the prints were meant for exhibition.

New coccine is a valuable retouching medium. It is a red dye which is purchased in powdered form and dissolved in water. The use of the dye is to hold back light from that part of the film you wish to appear lighter in the print, and with more detail. It is usually applied to the thinner parts of the negative. However, it is applied only to thinner parts which already have detail, not to merely transparent portions, as they would only print gray instead of black. With this medium, hair can be made to look lighter or to have more detail, the shadow parts of a garment can be brought out, or architectural detail in shadow can be made more evident. Here, too, practice is important. The trick is to get the dye on the local area evenly and gradually. A sable brush somewhat larger than the spotting brush is needed. First moisten the brush in clear water, then go over the area to be treated, brushing back and forth with a pushing motion as if to work the water into the gelatin emulsion. This is best done with the brush held at right angles to the negative. Enough of the powdered coccine has previously been dissolved in a small bottle of water to make a solution deep red in color. This stock solution lasts indefinitely. For a working solution, take a few brushfuls of the stock solution and put it into a small glass and add a little water so that the color of the liquid is pink instead of red.

Coccine is never brushed on evenly by one application. The knack is gradully to build up a number of coats of the pale pink dye, each time pushing the brush back and forth as evenly as possible, until an over-all evenness is achieved, and the density of the red dye deepens to the tone required. The brushing can be done on both sides of the film, so that if there is pencil work on the emulsion side, coccine can be applied on the celluloid side. The amount of brushing will depend on how light you want the area to appear in the print. It may be necessary to make a test print before you can be certain if enough coccine has been applied. The film is dried thoroughly before you print it. If you have not used enough coccine, begin again and add still more coats, or increase the amount of stock solution in the working solution. If you make a mistake, soak the film in a tray of water to which has been added a few drops of ammonia and wash it until the red disappears. Dry, and try again. The entire operation needs to be practiced for you to become proficient. Usually, difficulties arise from using the diluted coccine too strong and thus starting out with a badly streaked and uneven tone. As in any phase of photographic retouching, patience is needed, first of all.

A new formula which has come on the market recently is the Carl Dial retouching fluid. It is applied directly to the print for local reduction, so as to lighten hair, eyes, clothes or any other part desired.

Cropping

Trimming the print is a further step in finishing the photograph. Ordinarily, it is to be hoped that the picture has been so well composed on the ground glass that no excessive cropping is necessary at this point. But since there are many factors to prevent the attainment of perfection, cropping is frequently called for. Certainly, edges which do not contribute to the unity of the picture or which detract from the center of interest or divide interest should be cropped. Likewise, the shape of the subject may not always fit the standard dimensions of the negative, as explained in the chapter on composition. Very often, the print must be trimmed so that vertical lines are not tipped. This is true when the camera was not leveled off straight at the time of taking the picture. If a hand camera has not been held straight, too often important corners in a print must be sacrificed to straighten the vertical lines. Horizontally directed lines more or less take care of themselves, in fact are more likely to be diagonally placed. But if vertical lines are not upright, an uneasy, unbalanced effect is created, which produces a feeling of psychological insecurity. When the camera has been pointed upward, vertical lines converge. In this case, the convergence must at least be equalized, not toppling over to one side. Slightly converging lines which are symmetrically placed can be straightened up in enlarging by tipping the easel. Where a frankly tipsy angle shot is made, it is assumed that the angle has been well thought out and balanced in its own right and that the subject naturally calls for such an angle to create a definite emotional effect or meaning. Sometimes technical problems in taking the picture —the sun being in an unfavorable position or possibly hiding behind a house, or lack of space preventing you from withdrawing to a suitable distance—force the photographer to make an angle shot.

A good trimmer is needed, whether for routine trimming or cropping. It should cut squarely and sharply and be so constructed as not to warp. Since a trimmer is permanent equipment, it is wise to buy a good one. Care is important, too, and a main point is not to cut heavy cardboard on the trimmer; for this dulls the knife and throws the tension out of adjustment for photographic paper. Follow the maker's instructions for maintenance and care. Rather than buy a poor trimmer, it is better to make shift with a straight edge and a razor blade. To protect yourself, use the type of blade which has a rounded back, or if you use a double-edged blade, tape one side. If you cut with a straight edge and sharp blade, it is advisable to place a sheet of zinc under the print for the knife or blade to cut into, the metal needing to be of a character hard enough for a clean edge and soft enough not to dull the cutting edge. Of course, if you only mat your photographs, this consideration is not urgent. For composition, whether you use mounts or mats, it is a good practice to make two L-shaped pieces of white cardboard and move them about over the print to see the final result before trimming or cutting a mat. With enlargements, of course, the final composition is decided on the easel, and only the edges of the print are trimmed later.

19. Presentation

WHEN the finished photograph is mounted for presentation, the laws of composition are carried one step further. Injudicious placing of a print on its background, whether mount, mat or frame, can seriously detract from the visual weight of a picture. Inharmonious colors may alter the subtle tonal values of the black-and-white print—throughout our discussion we have been talking chiefly about black-and-white photography. Texture of papers used for mounts or mats is another item to consider seriously. Finally, if photographs are framed, there is the question as to what type of molding is suitable for the rather severe, certainly not antique character of the medium. Here, again, taste will determine how your photographs are presented. But taste is not an inherited characteristic, like the color of your eyes; it is developed through experience and cultivation and to a large degree it reflects the standards prevailing in a period. The drive of our period is toward a method of presentation congenial to the spirit of modern photography.

Mounts or Mats

To begin with, mounts of suitable tone must be chosen, to match the tone of the print. In other words, a black-and-white print should not be mounted on a cream colored paper; for this will have the effect of making the white look dirty. Even so-called white mounts vary considerably in tone, being yellowish, bluish, pinkish, grayish, greenish, or what have you. Pure whites are rare and are most easily obtained in the most expensive mount or mat boards, unfortunately. If you have standardized your printing paper fairly well, you can buy mounts which best match the particular color of that paper. As the tone of the mount can either brighten and enhance the effect of a print or rob it of its fullest visual effectiveness, best take prints with you when you select mounts.

Whether you mount your prints on top of the support or mat them behind a cutout paper mat, the problem of the relation of physical materials is about the same. The choice between mounts and mats is, however, a rather more complicated esthetic one. It involves a feeling for the spatial relations of picture and the plane which separates it from the wall on which it is hung. Essentially, the function of a mount or mat is twofold: to protect the print from handling and to enhance its visual message. The protective function may be fulfilled in many ways; the esthetic function of enhancement is best carried out when the photographer has a keen sense of the meaning of his pictures and how he wants them to speak. There are valid arguments for standardization of presentation, if prints are to be widely exhibited in group exhibitions; the arguments for individual presentation are just as valid, if the photographer wishes to make every part of the photograph completely an expression of his own idea. Thus when the Museum of Modern Art exhibited Barbara Morgan's dance photographs, color was an organic part of the installation, as a visually physiological way of calling attention to the pictures themselves.

Carry this logic further, and you come up against the question of mounts vs. mats. My personal preference is for mounts; as I feel that the photograph is the cleancut, straightforward projection of a picture to the eye, and the spatial relation between the photograph and the mount seems to me to serve this quality of projection better than imprisoning the picture behind the cutout mat. There is a hangover of oldtime esthetic snobbishness about the mat, harking back as it does to rare prints and the portfolio psychology of collectors, who put up drawings and prints in fancy frames, with tinted mats and gold lines drawn around them. The photograph, being modern and rational, should not associate itself with this traditional folderol. The great argument for mats, of course, is that they can be more easily renewed than mounts, and therefore the life of the exhibition print is longer and the photographer does not sink so much labor and materials in preparing photographs for exhibition purposes. On the wall in the home, I like to feel that the photograph comes off the wall a little, as it does when mounted on top of its paper support, rather than feel that I have to probe back into the wall to see the picture. Actually, the dividing line here may be whether you think of photography as "art" like etchings, aquatints, etc., or whether you believe it to be a medium in its own right, with its own standards of quality and presentation.

Mounting

Where prints are likely to be handled a great deal, as in museums, schools, libraries, they may better be mounted on dark-colored mounts which will not show handling. The Russell Sage Foundation Library has done this with the collection of Hine photographs they purchased shortly before Hine's death last year. For such uses, the prints should be mounted so as to be easily removable when the mounts need to be renewed. If they are kept in albums, they can be tipped in with rubber cement or similar adhesive, the pressure of the closed pages being depended on to keep them from curling.

For temporary display, prints may be mounted with rubber cement. Of course, this is not a permanent method and may even finally discolor the print; but if the operation is carried out neatly and carefully, the job may last several years. The rubber cement is spread on both print and mount, with care being taken that sufficient cement is spread around the edges so that the print will lie flat. The print is then firmly pressed down over the entire surface with a clean cheesecloth and placed under pressure, as a heavy weight or in a dry mounting press. When the cement has set, excess adhesive is wiped off and brushed away, coming off in crumbs and leaving no mark.

Whether you mat or mount your prints, you will do well to back them first. This is better done with dry mounting tissue or Foto-Flat, though rubber cement may also be used if you are willing to run the risk of discoloration of the print after some years. For backing prints, probably the best material is a discarded print or a piece of stale photographic paper which has been fixed and washed. The reason is that the two pieces of paper, print and backing, have equal tensile strength, being of similar materials and both having been coated with the photographic emulsion, which exerts a pull, causing the paper to curl inward slightly. Print and backing are placed back to back and cemented together, so that these two pulls neutralize each other. If you are planning to mat your prints, do not trim the mounted photograph. There is another point to watch out for: the gelatin emulsion of the backing will not "take" to any adhesive, so you must first roughen it with sandpaper or steel wool, and then tip it on by the corners to a cardboard. The cutout mat is then placed over the print, carefully cut to size of the photograph as it is to appear finished, including any necessary cropping of edges.

Foto-Flat is a popular method of mounting today. Sheets of the adhesive membrane are tacked to the back of the print by means of a warm Fotowelder, or a household electric iron will do. The sheet of Foto-Flat and the print are then trimmed together and tacked in place on the mount, again with the Fotowelder or the electric iron. Place a sheet of clean paper over the print, and pass the moderately warm Fotowelder or iron over the surface to heat the gum of the adhesive membrane. Then place mount and print under a weight, and as the Foto-Flat cools, the print will be found to adhere firmly to the mount.

Dry mounting of prints is the most permanent and professional method. Dry mounting tissue is a sturdy transparent sheet, permeated with shellac. It is tacked to the back of the print in two or three places with a tacking iron. Print and tissue are then trimmed together and tacked on the mount. The dry mounting press is a machine heated with electrical units, which provides both heat and pressure to seal print and mount in a practically indissoluble union. More heat is needed than for Foto-Flat, the sealing taking place at from 15 to 60 seconds and at a temperature from 175 to 200 degress Fahrenheit. Thin cardboard is placed over the print to protect its surface from the heat of the electrically heated metal surface. If any moisture has remained in the print or mount, the print will not adhere permanently. If the dry mounting press gets too hot, the print also will not adhere. The great advantage of dry mounting, besides the fact that the print lies absolutely flat, is that it seals off the back of the print and prevents physical deterioration from setting in from the back.

A method which permits the mount to be renewed is first to dry mount the print on a thin sheet of bristol board or on a piece of photographic paper as described above and then, after trimming, to tip the print onto the mount with an adhesive like rubber cement. If the mount becomes discolored or broken at the corners, it may be replaced without losing the print, an important item if you exhibit widely.

Format

Three factors control the best presentation standards, namely, color of mount, texture of mount and appropriate placing of the photograph in the format of the mount. Rough surfaces make a print look smoother, smooth make it look rougher. A large head with a great deal of texture looks smooth on a rough board, as do enlargements with any degree of grain, while the texture and detail of a fine finished print may be enhanced with a smoother mount. If possible, stock two types of mounts, to be used according to subject and its treatment.

Placing the print in its proper space creates interesting problems. Here again, set rules do not apply, the individual print sometimes calling for special handling. Traditionally, we can start with the proposition that the photograph should be placed on its mount or mat in a manner comparable to book page design, the top margin being the smallest, the side margins wider, and the bottom margin the widest. The theory behind this traditional spacing is that equal margins would be monotonous. The reasons behind the convention are many and complex. The usual proportions of book pages in the days of the scribes were determined by the shape of vellum, which in turn depended on the shape of the sheep it came from. A long, relatively narrow page resulted. When papermaking mills came into Europe in the fifteenth century, paper followed the tradition of vellum. The invention of printing and the spread of books still was influenced by these historical facts. Even today, paper sizes (made by machinery instead of the old handcraft methods) are controlled by tradition, and book format continues to follow precedent, though there is no particular esthetic warrant for the long, narrow page. Prints, whether of the older graphic arts medium or of photography, have also been affected by these conditions. Now, however, there is a trend away from the rectangle toward the square, in such German cameras as the Tenax, Ikoflex, etc., and in typographical design for photographic books, as in the catalogue of the Walker Evans exhibition at the Museum of Modern Art in 1939. The more nearly square format is more sympathetic to space design as we understand it in this period, and as it has been conceived by such a contemporary abstractionist as Mondrian.

However, when you try to buy mounts or mats, you will run up against tradition in a rigid mood. Mounts and mats are standardized to the old-fashioned sixes of 14 x 10 or 16 x 20, and it is difficult to get other proportions except by buying paper and having it cut to the size you want. This is not impossible, as papers do come in other sizes than the standard book paper sizes, notably the "elephant" which can be cut to good advantage. I have used a 14½ x 17 inch mount, which I like for general shape. A note: modern practice requires all prints, whether vertical or horizontal, to be mounted with the mount or mat vertical.

If you exhibit very much, of course you may find yourself confronted by the tyranny of custom; for museums set up specifications of sizes which meet their installation facilities or the glass they have on hand or some other similar external condition. Then you will simply have to mount or mat your prints as specified. However, I feel that the reform in these matters is long overdue and hope that photographers will bring it about before long.

In placing the print on the mount, generally, it is wise to follow a moderate style, that is, one in which the print is centered, though the top margins or the bottom margins need not be the same for all subjects. However, prints can be bled on all four sides, on three sides, on two sides, or one side, and in all kinds of space arrangements. They can even be placed diagonally on the mount, if there is any reason for doing so. They can be placed off center, if that seems to emphasize the compositional pattern. The advantage of tipping them on, as described in the last paragraph in the section on "Mounting" is that it gives you leeway to experiment this way. Extreme placing, however, is distasteful if the unusal arrangement is not called for by the movement or the meaning of the picture. The large exhibition of Lewis Hine's photographs, held at the Riverside Museum in 1939, showed asymmetrical and untraditional mountings to good advantage.

In the main, simple mounting is certainly preferable to bizarre, the mount acting as a background to the print, to bring out its qualities to best advantage. Nothing in mounting should distract attention from the photograph. For this reason, I strongly oppose borders, embossed edges, double mounts, lines inscribed around the print, in short all the fancy paraphernalia invariably used to conceal the poor photograph. The commercial ornate folders are to be avoided like the plague. If manufacturers still insist that the taste of photographers is pathetic, it is up to photographers to clear their good name, by shunning all but the simplest mounts. There are few, if any, stock mounts worth considering, and photographers will just have to have recourse to intelligence and ingenuity, searching out stores with good stocks of paper, and planning their own presentation.

There are other ways of protecting and preserving photographs for display. Varnishing and waxing serve to enhance the paper quality of the print. Clerc (Section 714) gives directions for this. The drawback is that the varnish or wax often turns yellow and so detracts from the original "color" of the print. About two years ago, I had some enlargements of mine (20 x 24 and 24 x 30) mounted on masonite, bled to the edges, and sprayed with a matte lacquer by air-brush. These prints have traveled a fair amount, been hung a number of times, and handled considerably; yet they have stood up very well. Paper today does not have the material richness of the old gold chloride or platinum paper; but the lacquering seems to have the effect of making the prints richer and more luminous.

A further note: displaying photographs in the home creates a problem. Shall you have dozens of favorite prints framed at a fair cost to yourself, and then ever after face the difficulty of finding storage space for them? A modern device like the Braquette, which sells for $1, is a satisfactory solution. In my own studio, I worked out a panel for the display of photographs, which consists of a back and moldings screwed into the wall. The top molding is hinged and lifts up, so that prints can be changed easily. When it is clamped down, it holds a piece of plate glass firmly in place over the photographs. In this way I get variety and at the same time a sense of permanence.

20. Portraiture

COUNSEL is a dangerous thing; for portraiture means many different things to different people. To clarify confusion, we may start out with "What does it mean to you?" Portraits range all the way from the most casual snapshops to *chichi* surrealist concoctions. They can be out of focus, inane, sentimental, disguised versions of the person, masquerades. Or they can be a real revelation of the person, the inner life and quality revealed through face, through pose and attitude of body, though characteristic gesture, dress and environment.

Portraits require an even more strenuous re-education of the eye than other kinds of photography. When all is said and done, photography is essentially a medium in which the eye must be coordinated and trained to see as the lens sees, to know what it has really seen and what it wishes to express. As a dancer's muscles and grace are developed by dancing, so the photographer's ability to see creatively grows as the eye is trained and becomes ever more acute, penetrating and inclusive. When a subject strikes a responsive visual chord, the photographer's many sets of eyes come into focus. He sees the subject itself; but at the same time he sees behind, above, in front of and to the side of the subject simultaneously. Complex, indeed, is the vision of the trained eye.

Apply this vision to the problem of making portraits, and what do we find? The maker of great portraits will have to have a burning curiosity which probes beneath the flesh to the bone and beyond that to the soul of his sitter. He may romanticize or dramatize a person, but in no petty spirit. The essence of the portrait is humanity, its meaning, all its thoughts, emotions, characteristics. How a person's life speaks through his eyes, the modeling of his cheekbones, the weight of his body as he sits or stands, are subtle nuances, without which portraiture is mechanical and lifeless. In my

54. JAMES JOYCE, PARIS, 1928 — BERENICE ABBOTT

Taken with 13 x 18 cm. view camera with 9 x 12 cm. reducing back; f/4.5 Hermagis lens.

55. JULES JANIN NADAR

portrait of Atget, I sought to evoke the weariness of this indefatigable photographer of Paris, as if the slump of his shoulders visibly symbolized the labor of thirty years tugging about his bulky 18 x 24 cm. view camera and heavy glass plates. In fact, it was a disappointment to me when he appeared at my studio dressed in his "best" suit, instead of in the patched, stained clothes I had always seen him wear before.

The qualities to be sought in portraiture are three: a good likeness, character and spontaneity. Of course, most people indulge in a certain amount of self-deception. They imagine they want to see themselves as they really are; yet their subconscious censor shears away double chins, warts, big ears, and such, so that their mental image is totally different from what the outsider sees, and especially from what the relentless lens registers. Here what the photographer must do is to put the sitter's best face forward, without sacrificing all identity.

Truly, portraiture has a tradition which today takes living up to. The early daguerreotypes, calotypes and photographs are remarkable for their qualities of honesty and acute observation. To be sure, the excellent likenesses found in them are partly due to the slowness of lenses a century ago and the resulting depth of field obtained in the pictures. But the portraits of Hill, Nadar and Julia Margaret Cameron, to mention the three stars of nineteenth century portraiture, are noteworthy not for technic or lack of technic, but again because of the man (or the woman) behind the camera. Despite difficulties, these artists with the camera captured what it takes to make a good portrait, likeness, character, spontaneity. Mrs. Cameron's portraits have a spontaneity, which is as candid as the miniature camera, while Nadar's two portraits are certainly excellent statements of character. When we begin to analyze the value of photography, we really need to look back a little and see what was achieved with slow lenses and clumsy machines.

There are two schools of thought in regard to portraiture, which may be described as informal and formal. In the informal may be included outdoor shots, where natural lighting simplifies the problem to an extent, and indoor shots in casual, everyday surroundings, where extra artificial lights are needed, usually with small fast hand cameras and flashlights. The formal comprises portraits done under studio conditions, with a ground glass camera on tripod, photofloods and studio lights, and a slower, more carefully studied method of working. Actually, portraits outdoors may move into the formal class, in Hill's masterpieces *The Finley Children* and *The Cockburn Family*, while Gay Dillon's *Tom* (Pl. 51) is a simple illustration of informal portraiture with no frills, as also in *Portrait of a Writer* and *Portrait of a Painter*, here shown. As far as candid portraits with flash are concerned, you will simply have to apply the technical information presented in the next two chapters to the especial problems of portraiture. The drawback to this type of portrait is that the small cameras do not permit you to "draw" your subjects, as you can with the ground glass camera.

In discussing studio portraits, my approach is not so much a genre one, as what perhaps might be called "pure portraiture," by which is meant, character, personality, expression, all the little things which differentiate one person from another. The face as the focus of personality is the main motive in portraiture, ninety per cent of the time. However, a person may be revealed in many other ways, as in Russell Lee's *Old Woman's Hands* (Pl. 12) or my *Hands of Cocteau* (Pl. 17) and *Eyes of Audrey McMahon* (Pl. 30). Perhaps the best portrait ever made of me showed my feet in "Mopassins." Generally, the face deserves most attention and should be truthfully presented, in all its plastic complexity of structure and modeling. Four factors are involved:

1. *Mechanical:* Distance of sitter from background, distance of tripod from sitter, and height of tripod.
2. *Lighting:* to model the features and the planes of the face.
3. *Creative:* establishing an affirmative relation with the sitter.
4. *Processing:* the kind of negative you aim for in portraiture.

I have called the first consideration "mechanical," because it concerns external spatial relations between subject, room or what, camera, and photographer. Keeping in mind that the purpose of a portrait is to capture the sitter's personality at the height of characteristic spontaneity, do not choose a background likely to detract from the person or to dissipate the human interest. The background should enhance the person, not be the whole picture, like a Victorian painting of a parlor in which attention is delighted by the furniture and drapes and ignores the people. Thus, if the interior of a room is chosen, make sure that no conspicuous objects like lamps, doorknobs, bookcases, potted palms, project from the subject's nose or ears. You would not photograph Einstein against an "ad" for Vaporub in a subway car, unless of course you sought to carry the laws of relativity to a far-fetched imaginative comment.

Under studio conditions, general rules may be stated. The sitter should not be too close to the background. There should be plenty of space to place lights in back of the person as well as in front, which means that the wall or background should be at least three feet away. This point is important also, because it is desirable to give a sense of air around the human figure, so that it is visualized as a solid, three-dimensional volume in space. This does not mean that you cannot place a sitter with his head leaning directly against a brick wall if you so desire; but in that case, make sure that the texture and lighting of the wall does not steal interest from the person.

Furthermore, the tone of the background should be adjusted to the general tone of the subject. Do not have the background the same tone as the flesh or the clothes. A plain light colored wall can always be made to serve and, of course, the tone of a light wall can be varied by lighting and also by the distance the sitter is placed away from the wall. If you wish the background darker, move the sitter farther away. Varying tones can be produced by throwing a spotlight on the background. This applies to portraits taken in the sitter's home. Usually it is wiser to simplify the setting, although a good portrait in which the person is seen in habitual surroundings is not to be sneezed at. The reason I advise against it is that you may concentrate so much on the setting that the person is lost in the hypo.

The next mechanical step is to set up the tripod at the proper distance from the sitter. Do you want a true likeness? Then place the camera nine feet away, if at all possible. This is a much debated point, and many photographers deliberately get too near in order to get a bigger image on the negative. Obviously, it is desirable to have as big an image as possible so that necessary retouching may be done on the negative; likewise, it is almost impossible to retouch a very small head. But if you approach too near your subject, you are bound to get optical distortion which subtly falsifies the likeness. A stuffy, leathery, swollen mass results, instead of true drawing of the face; and the sensitive eye can sense the distortion even if you cannot explain it. Distortion is less likely with profiles, since the features are more nearly in the same plane. Only the experienced photographer can distort just enough to gain his effect, without losing it. Sometimes a dramatized version of character or physiognomy is more important than likeness; but this does not come under direct portraiture. Ralph Steiner's portrait of "Schnozzle" Durante is a classic example of distortion for effect.

Because a big image is needed for retouching and a safely adequate distance from the sitter is imperative for good drawing, a lens of relatively long focal length is your logical choice. A Cooke portrait lens or a Voigtländer Heliar is ideal for portraits. A further argument for long focal length is that if the camera is placed too near the figure, it tends to fatten up the sitter.

Next on the agenda is the camera's height. Good results require that the height be varied with each sitter. In the majority of cases, the camera is best placed at eye level or a little higher. If the camera is too high, the effect is to shorten the head, to exaggerate a bald spot, or to weaken an already receding chin. The jaw line is important and should be studied for best drawing. Raising or lowering the camera can clean up the jaw line or give indiscreet glimpses of voluminous chins, delicately rippling. If the neck is short, chin weak, nose too long, the camera should be placed lower to compensate. On the other hand, if you wish to accentuate a fine set of nostrils, place the camera lower, not for compensation, but for emphasis. As nearly all faces are asymmetrical, it is desirable to study both sides of the subject's face in order to photograph its more favorable side. Each face should be carefully though quickly analyzed, and your decision as to camera height made then. Practice, practice, and the eye strengthens its vision!

Background, distance of sitter from background, height of camera all settled, the next consideration is to place the image on the ground glass with ample space about it—crowding is fatal—and with due thought for the direction in which the sitter is looking or, better still, the direction in which the body faces. Before you think about lighting, it is well to seat your subject in a comfortable position with the body approximately posed as you expect to take the picture, the final posing waiting till the last instant before making the exposure.

First "must" for portrait lighting is: let the light be soft and diffused. Examine faces under direct light and under diffused light, and you will see a marked difference in the quality of flesh. Lights must not be so strong or harsh as to make the eyes strain and blink, as if the sitter were being put through the third degree. The best guide for portrait lighting is to observe light on the human face as it falls naturally from many sources, such as lamps, windows, the sun. Otherwise, lighting is to be considered for its ability to model the features to best advantage. Guard against unpleasant shadows around the nose and eyes. High foreheads should not be too strongly high lighted or weak chins photographed in a tapering-off light. Planes in a face are interesting and need to be stressed by the way you place your lights.

You will need one general light of fairly high power, such as a No. 2 photoflood, or several No. 1 photofloods. Whatever your main light source, have it as strong as possible without paralyzing the sitter's eyes. For in portraiture perhaps more than in any other kind of photography, you are truly "painting with light." However, when I took Joyce I could not use any lights, because of his bad eyesight, and simply had to hope for the best. In photographing the painter Eilshemius, I had an even more difficult problem. Not only could I not use light—the house not being wired for electricity, but lighted with gas—but Eilshemius was ill, deaf and shaky. I could not yell at him to keep still, for he could not keep still even if he heard me. What was I to do? Just pray.

Your main light, assuming you are not dealing with special problems like Joyce and Eilshemius, must be diffused and also reflected back onto the shadow side of the subject; or a secondary light must be placed so as to light up the shadow side. If high lights or accents are wanted, additional lights (spotlights or even the little Birdseye bulbs used for theatrical flood-lighting) may be used. To lighten the hair or dark parts of the clothing. If you do not lighten the shadows, they will come out almost black. To avoid this, resort to a reflector, a simple piece of white cardboard doing the trick if nothing else is at hand. In lighting the hair, watch out for unwanted high lights on the tip of the nose or the ear. You can tell better how the lighting looks from the ground glass than by eye until you have trained your eye thoroughly. When back lighting the subject, be sure no light rays strike directly on the lens. Cheekbones are important and may be emphasized or minimized, according to the general drawing of the face, by the way in which the secondary lights are arranged. When using auxiliary spots, remember that a front light is likely to make a person look older. A low light like stage lighting is flattering to the eyes.

To eliminate unpleasant shadows, throw a light directly on the background. Contrariwise, dramatic shadows can also be projected on the background if you study the composition and see what the shadows do to the whole picture, *including* what is after all the center of interest, the sitter! Generally, lights should be fitted with diffusers, such as the excellent professional ones of spun glass. Less expensive are buckram screens, which are placed at some distance from the light source, giving even, soft light, though at some cost in loss of strength of light.

In modeling the features, move the lights about, holding the reflector at different heights. Lighting is different for every face, and you will learn to adapt it to the person. However, if you want lighting to be perfect, you have to sacrifice some spontaneity. That is why I prefer simple lighting. There has to be a choice: perfect technic or perfect expression; rarely do you get both. My choice is perfect expression. It is desirable to combine both as much as possible; but it is harder to portray, or reveal, character than it is to get the light just right. When you begin to work for character, you enter the creative side of portraiture. You have to win the confidence of your sitter, get that person to relax, to feel at ease, at home. You want naturalness, and you may even have to employ tricks to get a natural and characteristic expression of countenance. You have to talk to the sitter and draw him out, establish a personal, human relation, which is friendly and warm even though temporary.

This is a last minute consideration, however. Before you can even think of creating a rapport with the sitter, you have to do a few practical but very necessary things, such as get the subject placed on the ground glass and get it sharp. *Always focus on the eyes.* Who called them "the window of the soul?" Then, study the image to see if the rest of the figure is in focus. Use the swings to bring them into focus, if possible. In portraiture, the creative and the technical are thoroughly scrambled. For example, I have just written that between perfect technic and perfect expression, I take the latter. Now perfect expression is matter of split seconds; so the fastest film you can get is an added help.

Lastly, the sort of negative needed for portraits is to be considered. Because of artificial lighting and relative nearness of the camera, portraits are contrasty as subjects, just as sun falling in a deep woods is a very contrasty subject. But the negative you want is a soft negative because the contrastiness in portraits is only what the lens sees. To the eye, human flesh, skin and hair are soft and warm. By nature and by vision, portraits are soft subjects, though according to optics they are contrasty. To compensate for this optical contrastiness, you have to give full exposure and minimum development, first balancing your lighting to bring out all the roundness and softness of your subject. To estimate exposure, do not consider merely the head, but take a reading from the darkest area of the clothes, where texture is important. Only in fashion work, do you need to have light accents fully in the clothes. For portraiture generally, clothes should be lighted with an eye to characterization.

21. The Miniature Camera

THIS chapter offers a brief summary of the uses of the miniature camera as a specialized field of photography. Apart from its scientific applications, for which the 35 mm. camera is admirably suited, the field in which miniature camera work excels and truly finds its perfect function is "candid" photography. Today candid photography means all things to all people, the scope of the miniature camera having been artificially widened to include functions which logically belong to other types, so that we find thousands of minicam fans trying to do with the miniature camera what can only properly be done with the "big" camera or at least with a ground glass camera. The practice of Eliot Porter of photographing birds with a small view camera is an excellent refutation of the mistaken idea that action cannot be taken with anything except the 35 mm. machine.

When Dr. Barnach designed the first miniature, the Leica, in 1913, he seemed to be perfectly aware of its function and place. He photographed people in the streets without their knowledge, took them in natural positions, with natural expressions, doing things that were characteristic of their ordinary activity. In most cases, this meant a close-up or semi-close-up, of people being taken off guard. Later on, the idea grew up (almost like Topsy) that candid meant solely embarrassing shots such as a man eating spaghetti and dribbling, looking like a scared camel, or what have you, of sleeping drunks sprawled out in a subway car, of human beings at their most unguarded moments, pathetic, grotesque or sinister. But as far as I can see, candid photography was, is and shall be, primarily for the purpose of capturing human, spontaneous expression and action, a glorious goal in itself. It need not be—and should not be, if photography is anything more than a game—a prying and peeping into life; it should be a revelation of the immediacy of human action and emotion, not a negative, destructive, scornful intrusion. However, what your idea of candid and human is rests with you. After all is said and done, it is the mind behind the camera which makes the camera count. Whether your choice and observation be one of depth or triteness depends on you, not the camera.

The only catch is that this glorious goal of human interest and significance is difficult to attain! So difficult, indeed, that in the large exhibitions of hundreds of prints from miniature films, the onlooker is lucky if he finds a half dozen truly candid shots, the subjects for which the miniature camera is fitted. The reason is that the miniature camera had a mushroom growth in this country, being promoted as the universal panacea of the photographer's ills. When the 35 mm. camera was introduced to the United States in 1923, there was no official welcoming committee to launch it as the white hope of photography. Not till the thirties, in fact, did it succeed in capturing attention and imagination.

Then it took like wildfire, like a Mississippi bubble or a Western boom. Photographers spent sleepless nights, thinking life would be unlivable without one, to the tune of $300. Back in the minds of many lurked the notion that here was an easy road to photography. Away with bulky ground glass cameras, no more wearisome chores toting tripod, plateholders and all. The minicam was small enough to tuck away in the pocket, almost like a fountain pen or a cardcase. In fact, I had a coat made to fit my first miniature camera (a Leica, though I now use a Contax) and planned to have the camera always by my side. The whole idea appealed to technology-minded Americans until the miniature camera became a craze. Manufacturers came out with countless models, most of them worthless. Furthermore, since the fad became one of contagion more than of reason, miniature cameras strayed from their basic powerful function of candid photography and became conspicuous in design. Instead of little, black cameras, they blossomed forth in burnished chromium, pretty to look at, visible a mile off, scaring away possible victims.

Yet in spite of dangerous distractions from the fundamentals of miniature work, the basic value of the miniature camera remains. The advantages are as pronounced today as ever before; likewise the disadvantages. The advantages are lightness, compactness, rapidity of operation, adaptability to bad light, good depth of field because of short focal length lens, hence particular suitability to all types of night and poor light subjects. The disadvantages are costliness, added expense for an enlarger, lack of all adjustments, the additional care with which tiny negatives must be processed, and most of all the especial expertness of use needed, as perfection of focusing, exposing, and so forth.

It goes without saying, therefore, that the miniature camera succeeds better in the hands of the expert than in the hands of the beginner. Anybody just starting photography with a serious purpose who thinks that he wants to do miniature camera work would best learn the principles of photography first with a larger camera, because it is much easier, and graduate later on to the 35 mm. machine when he is qualified to make good use of it. A wide experience with many students has convinced me that this method is to be preferred to starting off your photographic life with one of those beautiful, costly, intricate, minutely machined cameras, which are supposed to have taken all the pain out of photography, but which have actually put it in.

A further word of advice has to do with tempo: as the miniature camera can be used at high speeds for fast action under poor light, so it in turn calls for a rapid tempo of operation. Usually, this tempo is acquired by starting at a slower speed of operation and working up, as in practicing scales. In fact, tempo is a far more important part of photography than people realize. The speed of reaction time, the speed of perception, the speed of working, all affect the result. The highest tempo of work is, of course, that of the press photographer, who is always working at a stretch, hemmed in on one side by the fact that he must not miss the subject and on the other by the ubiquitous deadline.

A brief outline of procedure for miniature camera work follows. I am limiting suggested formulas, not because there are not other good ones on the market, but because I wish to emphasize the need for simplification in practice. As far as processing is concerned, this refers to miniature film from 2¼ x 3¼ down to 1 x 1.

1. Camera must be kept in perfect mechanical order.

2. Camera must be kept spotlessly clean inside. Use a good soft brush and an ear syringe for blowing dust out of corners.

3. Camera must be held steadily. A chain tripod is recommended.

4. Button or cable release must always be pressed gently, not jerkily.

5. Thorough familiarity with camera is a prerequisite. Practice quickly changing the shutter speeds.

56. EUGÈNE DELACROIX (1798-1863) NADAR

57. PORTRAIT OF AN ARTIST — BERENICE ABBOTT

Deardorff Triamapro.

58. PORTRAIT OF A WRITER — BERENICE ABBOTT

Taken with 4 x 5 Graflex; sunlight and flash.
An example of informal portraiture.

59. NEAR THE BATTERY — ANSEL ADAMS

Taken with Kodak Ektra; 50 cm. f/1.9 Ektar lens; 1/25; f/2.8;
Panatomic film; Eastman DK20.

6. Make a habit of giving shorter exposures with larger apertures, and not closing down. Depth of field is not important in miniature camera work. Stopping action and catching human interest are important.

7. Use a sunshade, nine-tenths of the time, at the very least.

8. Use fine grain film, such as Agfa *Plenachrome* or Eastman *Panatomic X*.

9. Don't use a filter for candid work. Human interest rarely demands it, and the loss in speed is crucial.

10. Full exposure and moderate development are the best guarantee against grain. Remember, the denser the negative, the greater the grain; and the greater the negative's contrast, the greater the grain.

11. Have a good tank for development, such as the Nikor, M M (Miniature Marvel), F. R. Adjustable, or F. R. 35 mm. (See the reference given in Chapter 3.)

12. Have all containers and darkroom scrupulously clean.

13. Prepare all solutions before beginning work.

14. First soak film in distilled water in the tank for three or four minutes before developing, to prevent the possibility of air bubbles forming, also to promote even development.

15. Use a standard fine grain developer, such as Agfa 17 or Eastman D76 or DK20, at 65 degrees; or if your darkroom is over 70 degrees in temperature or the weather so hot that the 65-degree temperature is difficult to maintain, use Harvey's panthermic 777. In every case, follow the directions carefully.

16. Gently agitate the tank at intervals of about a minute throughout development to insure even action. *Above all, do not overdevelop.* In any case, use the same formula all the time and become thoroughly familiar with its results.

17. Use a hardening short stop bath between developing and fixing, to toughen the film so that it will not scratch easily. This step is important because tiny marks become major flaws in enlargements from miniature film. The following is a good formula for the hardening bath. Potassium chrome alum, 2 ounces; 28 per cent acetic acid, 3 ounces; distilled water, 1 quart. This makes a stock solution, which lasts well. For use, dilute 1 part to 3 parts distilled water, and use *only once.*

18. Immediately after pouring out the developer from the tank, without rinsing the film pour in the hardening bath. Agitate the tank gently and thoroughly, and then leave the film in the solution for 4 minutes.

19. Next pour in hypo, using Defender I-F, which can be bought in 1-quart, 2-quart and 1-gallon packages as "777 Fixer (I-F)." This hypo lasts well; but better use it for film only. Ten minutes should be sufficient time for fixing. However, if the film clears in 2 minutes, leave the film in the hypo only 6 mintes. In other words, let the film fix three times as long as it takes for the first apparent clearing.

20. Wash the film in the tank in running water. Be sure there are several changes of water during washing, which should be for the full 20 minutes.

21. Finally, rinse the film well with distilled water, still in the tank.

22. Do not leave the film any longer than is necessary in any of the solutions, including water, as the gelatin tends to swell and soften and so to create a tendency toward grain.

23. After thorough washing, the film is hung up to dry, and clips are attached to the bottom to keep it from curling.

24. Excess moisture is gently wiped from both sides of the film (to avoid watermarks) with clean cotton wrung out in water and used only once.

25. Even temperature, not too hot, should be maintained throughout the drying, else a "shoreline" may result. Also, the film should be hung up in as dustless a place as possible. Ideally, air conditioning is called for in miniature film processing.

26. As soon as the roll is dry, it should be cut up into separate films if larger than 35 mm. The latter size should be cut into strips of six exposures and placed separately in cellophane or glassine envelopes. Negatives should not touch each other or abrasion is likely to take place. Film should not be rolled up.

27. If negatives are developed to a low contrast, it is quite possible to find a paper of medium contrast giving the best prints. Papers with a slightly rough surface or "tooth" are suitable for enlargements from miniature film; for grain in the negative will be "absorbed" by the texture of the paper.

Miniature Cameras

The three miniature cameras in the 35 mm. class worth considering for serious work are the Contax, Leica and Eastman Ektra. They should be carefully compared for ease of loading, ease of operating control, and lens performance, before you buy one of the three. Although they are all excellent machines, they seem to cancel out in some ways, a desirable feature in one machine being balanced by a second desirable feature in another, all perfections not being incorporated in any one type. The Contax has beautiful simplicity of loading, with its controls streamlined, while its metal shutter lasts the lifetime of the camera. The Leica is very compact, a favorite with many, while the Ektra has a new lens which is the pride and joy of the Eastman Kodak Co. This lens is chemically treated to reduce internal reflection, which gives more speed.

Above all, if you use a miniature camera, do not use it just now and then. Take pictures by the hundreds, nay, thousands, practicing to make perfect. If you are interested in color, the miniature camera is particularly well suited to Kodachrome. It has many uses for science, too, as in microphotography and medicine. Excellent references for advanced miniature camera work are the *Leica Manual* and *Miniature Camera Work,* the latter out of print, but now being issued in a revised edition under the title, *Modern Camera Work.*

22. Action: Flash

THERE is scarcely a medium in which specialization counts for so much as photography. You may be able to photograph fashion subjects, gardens, dogs, architecture, superbly well; but that doesn't mean that you can turn around suddenly and make good lantern slides or snappy sports pictures. Each field you attempt should be pretty well mastered before you try another; for each has special problems and technics. No field, probably, requires actual experience more than action work. This is one place where "Learn by doing" is about the only possible way of becoming expert.

There are very few directions which can help you with action work. To be sure, whole books have been written on action alone, and there are excellent chapters in *Miniature Camera Work* and *Graphic Graflex Photography*. Yet, to be armed with good advice culled from the experience of others will not necessarily enable you to get good results. The best thing you can do is to take many pictures and determine your own best procedure from them. You will rapidly learn what not to do. My observation of students who take up action work is that they expect the camera to do all the work. Either they snapped the shutter a little too early or too late, missing that peak of activity and interest, that climax of motion, which only the photographer can select. Or they did not observe keenly enough, so that a conspicuous but irrelevant figure got in the way at just the wrong moment, which they did not even see as they clicked the shutter. Eternal vigilance is certainly the price of photography, if you do not want odds and ends straying into the picture. Here particularly a high degree of nervous and muscular coordination is needed, with quickness of thought, manual dexterity and such thorough familiarity with the camera's mechanism that its operation becomes almost automatic in response to highly discriminating and willed orders from the eye and the brain.

To begin with, you have infinitely more control and accurate vision if you have a fairly sound practicing knowledge of photography. Where possible, in order to be able quickly and surely to select a background, you need to be familiar with the particular brand of action you are photographing, slow, medium or fast. Learn to anticipate the moments of the highest tension, the peak of activity. I do not know of another place where intense awareness is so important unless it is on the firing line where either you shoot accurately or are shot. The keyed-up emotion of the photographer pursuing action at any price is like that tense, nervous skill of the surgeon operating, finely trained, poised for his own kind of action.

The essence of photographing action is to stop motion at its most significant, characteristic and expressive moment. Therefore, the nature of the movement must be studied, and wherever possible that momentary lag when motion is almost at pause should be utilized. Since film is still slow and lighting rarely perfect, these moments of apparent equilibrium when opposing forces seem for an instant to have brought motion to a standstill really save the day for action shots. A hackneyed example is the often photographed subject of a pole vaulter at the top of his vault, as his body seems to float over the crossbar. Sports subjects of all kinds may be thought of to illustrate the point—the hurdler in mid-air, the horse just over the hedge, the pitcher at the height of his windup before the ball leaves his fingertips, the golfer at the top of his swing, the tennis player reaching for the ball in his serve. Simple actions like a man walking or lighting a cigaret have this same phase of pause or lag, when the motion is arrested to the extent that it can be more easily stopped than at another phase of the cycle. A complicated example of the application of this principle is to be found in the dance photographs of Barbara Morgan (see bibliography) who has spent several years of intensive study on the problem, without resorting to the perhaps more mechanical aids of the stroboscope or high speed flash. Her practice has been thoroughly to familiarize herself with the form of the dance itself by repeated observation, then to seek to photograph still shots which are kinetic in spirit. The standard which has controlled her work and which may be set forth as a sensible one is not to attempt to freeze all action but to utilize movement blur where it creates the sense of one movement in transition to another.

As photography may be specialized into many fields, of which action work is one, so action work in turn may be broken down into a number of subspecialities with special study and skills. If you are photographing contemporary rapidfire sports, baseball, football, hockey, basketball, you need to use a different technic and equipment than for average, casual action. Taking dogs at dog shows is almost a subdivision of a subdivision; and when you come up against the nervous, highly bred pedigreed animals, you need to be a canine psychiatrist as well as a photographer to bring home the dog. Babies are a story in themselves, and are always wonderful; but to catch their high moments, patience and calm are needed. Devotees of horseflesh call out another side of photographic human nature, which in turn entails more knowledge, more equipment and more headaches for the photographer who practices photography for fun, not for business. If you wish to be as serious with your hobby as professional photographers are with their jobs, you can find specialized chapters on all these and other subjects in *Graphic Graflex Photography.*

Quality in the sense that it can be achieved by the big camera is not a primary objective of action photographs, although a few genuine artists do achieve it despite the great handicaps. To catch the subject with the proper degree of motion is the basic consideration, with an active balance between the frozen motion of the arrested action and that amount of movement blur to convey the visual sensation and kinesthetic emotion of movement. Simple technical criteria which will serve as a guide to this objective are listed here in order of importance.

1. Get the picture sharp. To overcome this difficulty is the plague of professional as well as amateur. A good range finder or Graflex type of mirror which permits seeing the image and following it through help solve the problem. Where movement is not great, it is better to close down and give a longer exposure in order to insure sharpness. In flash work (to be discussed later in this chapter) focusing is easier since the lens can be closed down.

2. With faster action, be careful to catch the whole figure or group. Don't let the subject escape the confines of your negative. If there are no obstacles between you and your subject, withdraw to a distance so that you will have more leeway to center your action; thereby, you will avoid losing a few heads, arms, legs or feet. Furthermore, at a greater distance, there is a better chance that the necessary short exposure will be sufficient.

3. For fast action, such as races, sports, dance, use a camera with a focal plane shutter. The favorite of news photographers is the Speed Graphic, chiefly the 4 x 5. However, for this work, the miniature camera with its excellent shutter and exceptionally fast lenses is often used, either solely or as a supplementary camera, where poor lighting conditions do not permit another camera to be used. Where larger cameras would be taboo, the miniature may be used because its size makes it relatively inconspicuous. For moderate action, cameras with front between-the-lens shutters are adequate. In fact, the majority of action subjects can be captured from 1/250 second down to 1/2, so that cameras of the type of Rolleiflex, Ikonta, Deardorff Triamapro, Linhof and many other hand cameras qualify.

4. Understand the nature of motion as it registers photographically. Three factors must be considered. First, the speed of action. Is a man walking slowly or rapidly, or is he running? The speed of a rowboat, a galloping horse, and a locomotive differs. Obviously, the faster the action the faster the exposure needed. Second, the direction of the motion in relation to the lens. This may be directly toward or away from the lens, diagonally or obliquely athwart the lens, or across the lens at right angles to its axis of sight. Exposure must be adjusted accordingly. If the action is across the lens, you need to give it a third of the exposure given motion toward or away from the lens. The third consideration is the distance of the camera from the action. A much shorter exposure is needed to stop action near the camera, say, within 10 feet, than is necessary if the action takes place 25 feet away from the camera. New York traffic photographed from a considerable height can be stopped at 1/25 second. From ground level, up close, 1/200 second is by no means too fast.

In every category of action work, range of exposure varies according to the speed of the particular action. In photographing the circus, for example, you can give exposures all the way from 1/25 to 1/1000 second. If a bulky slow bear is riding a bicycle, a 1/50 second exposure will do, whereas a bareback rider may need 1/400 second. Here again the eye must learn to discriminate.

With action photography, it is appropriate to consider flash. Indeed, many types of action work force the photographer to underexpose negatives, particularly when light is not favorable. Any action which takes place near the camera, such as intimate street scenes or shots of people in the news, is likely to be underexposed. Sports and news photographers must, therefore, include efficient flashlight equipment in their working kits.

Space does not permit a comprehensive survey of synchroflash work here, which is a whole book in itself; but I shall give a few general suggestions which apply simply to amateur photography. If you have not done any flashlight work, I suggest that you begin with one bulb until you are thoroughly familiar with the method. Then you can go on to multiple flash. The simplest and least expensive way to experiment is with so-called "open flash," which is not synchronized, the shutter of the camera being first opened, then the flash set off, and the shutter quickly closed. You need an electric extension cord about 25 feet long, with a push button fixture, and a socket with reflector. Place an ordinary electric bulb in the socket, and move the light about until you have ascertained the best angle for a single source of light. Superior results are had if the single flashlight can be reflected back onto the shadow side of the subject from a light colored wall or, better, a piece of white cardboard, held or placed so as to get the maximum reflection of light. Light reflected back like this has a diffused character which softens the photograph and gives it greater roundness.

Having found the right location for the flashlight, remove the bulb and put in a medium sized flash bulb, such as No. 2 Superflash. This should be diffused by placing a sheet of tissue paper over it, holding the paper in place with a rubber band or clips. The subject should remain in the same spot but can move freely as far as talking or lighting cigarets or such movements are concerned. At just the right moment, open the shutter, push the button, and quickly close the shutter. In open flash, the full lighting strength of the flash is registered, while average motion is stopped. There need be no blur in the photograph from movement during the short time while you open and close the shutter if the lens has been shut down to, say, f/16 and if the room is only normally lighted. Open flash can be extended to the use of two or more bulbs for more subtle lighting effects, if they are all connected to the same electrical circuit.

The simplest method of working with synchroflash is to use only one bulb in a reflector fixed on the camera and synchronized to the shutter. I think a warning is in order here because all types of camera are not designed and constructed so as to work well with the rather elaborate mechanism needed for synchroflash. The shutters of many small cameras are likely

60. SEA FOOD, MOMMA? GLADYS BELLOFF

Taken with 1¼ x 1⅝ Foth Derby; 1/25; f/8; Verichrome. This amusing shot by a 17-year-old high school senior was awarded first prize, pictorial section, fourth scholastic salon of photography of the American Institute, 1941.

61. SMOKE EATERS — JESS STRAIT

Taken with 4x5 Speed Graphic; 1/200 second; f/11; flash. The photograph was made during a four-alarm fire which gutted a wooden box factory on Hamilton Avenue, Brooklyn. Five bodies were found at the spot. Awarded first prize in feature class, sixth annual exhibition, Press Photographers' Association of New York, 1941.

62. CELEBRATION — Barbara Morgan

Jane Dudley, Sophie Maslow and Frieda Flier of the Martha Graham Dance Group. Taken with 4 x 5 Speed Graphic; 1/700 second; f/11; Zeiss Tessar; Kalart Sisto gun, with four No. 31 General Electric flash bulbs; Agfa Triple S cut film; Agfa 17 developer. Lighted from top with two bulbs overhead, one bulb at left to cast light on the legs, and fourth bulb directed at back wall, to give depth.

63. TRINITY CHURCHYARD — BERENICE ABBOTT

In this photograph it was necessary to stop action of traffic in the streets. Because the camera was high up, this was possible even with an 8 x 10 view at 1/25 second.

to be severely damaged by the forceful push of the electrically tripped plunger which sets off the flash bulbs. It is important to find out first, before buying the expensive equipment, if your own camera can safely be operated with the photoflash synchronizers on the market.

Ordinarily, the single bulb at the camera gives flat pictures so that only subjects of inherently interesting and exciting content survive the resulting monotony. But the field of action photography in which I see the synchronized single flash giving first rate pictorial results is when it is used with sunlight. Here, you can use the flash to great advantage and get variety of lighting effects, letting the sun act as back light, side light or top light, and using the flash bulb on the camera to bring out what would otherwise be hidden in deep shadow. For all kinds of street action at close range, the single bulb brings to life many a shot which would otherwise be hopelessly thin and contrasty.

Multiple flash with synchronized equipment such as the Kalart and Abbey outfits make use of two or more bulbs for more elaborate lighting and indoor work. Careful study of the manufacturer's directions is your best guide here. Technical data are listed and explained at length in *Synchroflash* Photography by Willard D. Morgan. The diagrams illustrating Eliot Elisofon's article on "Flash Photography" in the 1941 *U. S. Camera* annual are helpful for the analysis required in multiple flash for professional photography. Full exposure, determined by practice and experience, and light development hold particularly true in flashlight work. Results are often contrasty due to the nature of flashlight illumination; and if the lighting is not well balanced, some areas in the picture seem to catch most of the light, leaving the rest in shadow. These areas will be overdense and flattened out if development is not kept to its minimum time. My experience with multiple flash has been to discount exposure tables based on stated lighting power of flash bulbs and to take the photograph with the bulbs closer than the distance given in the tables and at longer exposures. These tables seem to me to be over-optimistic. As with all exposure tables, the best guide is personal experience with given equipment.

23. Color Photography

APART from technical considerations, the principles of picturemaking apply equally to color photography and black-and-white photography. Learning to see optically, composing the subject, heightening the expressiveness of your material, all these problems are the same. The added feature of color, however, creates new technical problems, perhaps the most urgent being processing. At this stage of the evolution of color photography, this is still a problem of the manufacturer, not of the photographer, which is probably a blessing in disguise, although all color film processing does not yet produce standard results. The reason is that color photography is still in its infancy, just beginning life. The fact that it is a very healthy and promising infant causes us to hope great things from it in the future. The prospect of good color photographs is so alluring that with a little imagination, we can visualize truly exciting results—some day.

Whether or not we are satisfied with color photography as it exists today depends on our standards and criteria of judgment. Some gleeful color fans exult over results which to others seem monstrosities. Essentially our perception of color and our emotional response to it are conditioned by two factors, physiological and psychological. The former comprises the complex structure and functions of the eye, as well described in Dr. Callahan's essay, referred to in Chapter 10; as the eye sees with a more accommodating and flexible vision than the lens does, so it sees color more subtly than the chemical composition of color film can register it. The latter involves not only seeing the color but the memory of color, as we have known it through our associations with art. Color in painting is quite a different proposition from color in photography. The physical character of pigment in paint differs radically from the nature of color in light, especially when registered in chemical elements. Thus when we judge the color photograph, we not only think of how the subject looked in nature, but we also remember how painters throughout the centuries have rendered similar subjects. The color photograph has to satisfy a double standard—fidelity to real life and a recognizable approximation to traditional art. Ultimately, of course, color photography will evolve its own esthetic (probably quite different from that of painting) as black-and-white photography has today an esthetic not to be confused with that of graphic art. Before this can happen, color photography has to solve many technical problems.

It seems to me that the failure of color photographs today to satisfy critical taste lies in the fact that the selection of color in subjects is ill-considered. As in black-and-white photography, too often the impossible is attempted. Generally, color photographs are not kept within the limitations of the medium at its present stage of evolution. Even the makers of color film warn us of its limitations: that good rendering of one color may throw another color off, that we cannot as yet reproduce complex combinations of colors with truth to nature. The reason is, among others, that three colors cannot represent all the colors we see. As a matter of fact, in the best color reproductions of paintings as many as 17 color separations may be used, which indicates the complexity of the problem of rendering color by photographic methods. Nevertheless, color enthusiasts rush in wishfully and try to include all colors of the rainbow, and usually colors of the most blatant character. Here, again, the factor of human intelligence and discrimination cannot be overrated.

I do not wish to imply that color photography is of no value. Even at this stage in its growth, it exerts great power in the advertising field when used by experts. It can be of even greater value in specialized fields, such as medicine, science and art teaching. Esthetically, however, its value and realization surely lies in the future. In fact, the growing popular interest in color may well prove a spur to technicology to improve methods and materials so that color photographs will satisfy the real human need for such sensuous enhancement of the picture. It is quite possible that if you have not already worked with color, you may be attracted to it in the not too distant future, particularly when the cost of color film comes down.

With this possibility in mind, it is well to buy new lenses which are truly color corrected. Transverse chromatic aberration, which causes soft definition at the edges of the film is to be avoided at all costs. In black-and-white photography, this aberration merely results in softening of definition, whereas with color work the different colors overlap. This leads to a chief requirement of color photography: great depth of field is needed in the lens; for parts of the photograph must not be carelessly thrown out of focus, else the above disagreeable overlaps of red, blue and green take place. The new Eastman Ektar f/3.7 107-mm. lens is designed with especial attention to the problem; it is used with the Kodachrome Professional film, 2¼ x 3¼ inches.

Miniature film is still the most popular size of Kodachrome, because at best color photography is an expensive business. Miniature is used not only because of the element of expense, but also because since color film is slow compared with black-and-white film, necessary depth of field and sharp definition are more easily obtained with the short focal length lenses used on miniature cameras. To aid in obtaining good definition, it is desirable to use an opening not larger than f/11. If this is not possible, arrange to use a plain black background to avoid a discolored out-of-focus background.

With color work, exposure must be well nigh perfect. This is another argument for the use of miniature cameras. Shutters need to be more precise than in black-and-white work. Since exposure meters, judgments, shutters *et al.* vary, how are you to get perfect exposures without considerable experimentation? In order to use your meter accurately for color work, careful notes must be made until you have established what film speed rating is the correct one for your meter. In color photography, the reading is not taken from the shadows—in fact, shadows should not be pronounced—but the reading is made from a neutral gray matte cardboard about five inches square. The meter should be held from three to five inches from the card. The light which falls on the cardboard is the same light illuminating your subject. The card should be held away from colored objects which would reflect colored light on it. Eastman gives as a basic exposure for normal subjects in full sunlight 1/25 second at f/6.3. Even after experience with color photography exposure is gained, it is best to give a series of three exposures, differing from each other by a factor of one-half stop. Photoelectric exposure meters should be checked and calibrated by the maker for accuracy before you start color work.

Light must be fairly flat. When you have considerable experience with color film, reasonable exceptions may be made to this rule: but generally

64. ART CLASS — BERENICE ABBOTT

Taken with 9 x 9 cm. Rolleiflex; 1/100 second; f/22; two synchronized flash bulbs, one at camera diffused, the second bulb as close as possible without getting within range of the lens.

65. ICE CREAM CONE — W. Arthur Evans

This candid shot, made with a miniature camera, illustrates how the lighter and more entertaining aspects of human interest may be captured with the 35 mm. machine.

speaking, lighting must be much flatter than for black and white, which is still the "shadow catching" branch of photography. Compared with the great contrast permitted in black-and-white photography, the contrast in Kodachrome film is relatively small. Instead of exposing for shadows as in black and white, in color work it is important to expose for high lights. Therefore, the range of brightness must be equalized. An example with artificial light may be given. First, arrange a general flat flood lighting. Then additional lights are used to give modeling and accents. Any strong shadows cast by these secondary lights must be relieved by lights so placed as to illuminate the shadow areas and eliminate strong contrasts. A meter is used to check up on the uniformity of illumination. The Weston Electrical Instrument Corporation suggests a method of measuring range of desirable brightness with their meter, to obtain proper exposure balance. Take readings from various parts of the subject. Then the range of intensity should not exceed 4 to 1. In other words, the strongest high lights should be no more than four times as bright as the darkest areas. For lights and filters, follow Eastman's directions.

Despite discouraging esthetic results from color photography, due to the physical and psychological reasons stated, the lure of color is so great that photographers continue to plunge into this new field regardless of cost and uncertainty. This drive of amateurs undoubtedly will lead to ever simpler methods, which is necessary before color photography can become a medium for the millions as black-and-white photography is. The essential technical background of color temperature, pH of developer, Kelvin degrees, color balance and the like has really nothing to do with the activities of photographers who make pictures for their own pleasure, any more than the complicated studies of linguists need be understood by the layman who is able to read and write quite well enough for his needs.

Aside from this elaborate theoretical setting, color photography has suffered another drawback. The Kodachrome transparency may meet all esthetic standards and gives a completely satisfying picture in color. Yet, there is a considerable difference between the pleasure gained in handling and putting a print up on the wall and simply viewing a projected picture in color or, even worse, seeing it tiny and imperfectly illuminated as the film is held up to the light. Aside from the cost of color film, the added expense of projection equipment enters into the balance sheet for color photography.

A simple, relatively inexpensive method of making color prints from Kodachrome has, therefore, been much needed. Methods like pigment-printing, imbibition and chemical toning are lengthy, complicated and difficult. To meet this need, a new printing method has been devised, the Iso Color Process (see Paul Outerbridge's article in *U. S. Camera* magazine, No. 15. Also Julius J. Wolfson's article "The Iso Color Process" in *Modern Lithography,* April, 1941). This process does not require the use of expensive apparatus or temperature-controlled darkrooms. It does not employ a long and involved technic. The time needed to make a print should be no more than 40 to 50 minutes. Iso Color's 9 steps certainly seem simplicity itself.

The process, essentially, consists of printing by contact or projection each of three color separation negatives on thin stripping film. The exposed film is then developed in the appropriate color developer, where positive monochrome images are produced. After fixing in bisulphited hypo, the unwanted silver is removed in a quick bleaching procedure so that only a transparent color image remains. The film is cleared and washed before being stripped off from its paper base. The three layers are super-imposed on each other, and the print is finished.

The status of color photography being what it is today, it is clear that color and black and white fill two separate needs. As yet, *all* subjects and effects are not better taken in color. Just as selection of subject matter is a major consideration in every field of photography, so is judgment needed to determine what type of subjects are better and more fully realized in color and what in black and white. In a similar way, still photography and motion picture photography are often confused. Each fulfils its own purposes. What is most important in motion pictures is motion, action. What is most important in color photography is the impact and message of color.

24. "Straight" Photography

"STRAIGHT" photography is one of the major storm centers of photography. About this word and about this school, there still rages considerable controversy, although the style itself is certainly old enough to have attained its majority. Indeed, it is not distorting truth to say that photography throughout its existence essentially has been "straight." Despite flaws of technical performance in early daguerreotypes and calotypes and despite an occasional personal deviation such as Julia Margaret Cameron's preference for a slightly out of focus lens, the photographs which have come down to us from the past century as indubitable masterpieces are remarkable for qualities which can only be described as truly photogenic—precision in the rendering and definition of detail and materials, surfaces and textures; instantaneity of observation; acute and faithful presentation of what has actually existed in the external world at a particular time and place. Brady's Civil War photographs could not make their intense emotional appeal if we had any idea in looking at them that they were doped-up fakes like Hearstian war "atrocity" pictures.

Straight photography is, thus, a major part of the inheritance of contemporary photographers. If we are proud to be photographers and aware of the honorable tradition we have inherited, this inherent character of photography is part of our equipment for using the medium. Actually, alas, too many photographers adopt a position which can be explained by analogy: they act as if photography had no past and almost no future, as if writers were to ignore all that had been written in a thousand glorious years of English letters, making a crass assumption that the language had been invented only yesterday and for their especial, individual benefit. In this respect, the kinship of photography to writing is marked. Both incur a handicap but at the same time gain strength from their dual function, of being languages of colloquial speech, as well as mediums for highly concentrated and meaningful communication.

The curious thing is that photographers of every kind, from the veriest amateur to the most highly skilled professional, accept the word "straight" as describing a particular attitude, yet almost no one if challenged could give an acceptable definition of the concept. Beaumont Newhall in his *Photography: A Short Critical History* writes:

". . . the functional spirit caught hold of the younger generation of American photographers. They became interested in the problem of 'straight' photography—by which is meant not only the production of unretouched prints from unmanipulated negatives, but an insistence on the utmost clarity and detail of the image. . . . Edward Weston (Plate 77) and his son Brett Weston, Walker Evans (Plate 62), Berenice Abbott (Plate 51), and Ansel Adams (Plate 52), belong to this group. Their work, like Atget's, is usually limited in its field, because their desire for precise detail necessitates small stops and consequently long exposures. Arresting fast action does not predominate in their work; its chief value lies in its remarkable analysis of the face of nature and of man's work, rather than of mankind.

"Paul Strand's photographs are of a different kind. Equally interested in 'straight' technique, through his choice of lighting and understanding of his subject, he brings out the lyrical quality of nature and of man. Texture and detail, while remarkably rendered, are subordinated to the whole. A brilliant technician, Strand uses every available photographic means to obtain the results he wishes. The very color of the final print is calculated as meticulously as its precise mounting on pure white cardboard. . . .

"The exponents of pure photography, in its contemporary sense, wishing to get every possible advantage from their medium, make their prints mostly by contact. . . . Necessarily the size of the picture is determined by the size of the plate; for large pictures a large camera must be employed. The 'straight' photographer also composes his picture on the ground glass viewing screen of the camera. The final image is unaltered, once the exposure has been made; 'cropping' or trimming of prints is to their minds wasteful and inappropriate."

To my mind, this description is somewhat too limited, placing as it does the emphasis on method rather than meaning. If we accept it, should we then say that "straight" photography is merely a *style*, whereas "documentary" photography is a philosophy? The century-long tradition to which I have referred suggests that straight photography is broader in its scope than the excesses of the f/128 school, wider than false purism. We may even argue that the fact that straight photography does not mean technic alone is proved by the work of photographers as vastly different as Cartier-Bresson and Doris Ullman, where a kind of anti-technic revolution, conscious or intuitive, grew up against technic without meaning or broad human emotion.

As I see straight photography, it means using the medium as itself, not as painting or theater. Straight photography should be understood, I believe, not as the product of a group of photographers but as a historical movement expressing the interplay of forces. It was a necessary revolt from the worst follies of pictorialism—manipulation of prints, toning, double printing, fuzzy imitation of inferior Corots. In passing, I might remark it is significant that the best informed opinion now rejects the Corot landscapes but elevates the more plastic and realistic figure paintings of his earlier period. In painting, even as in photography, the cycle of taste reforms itself.

I have written that photography has always essentially been a straight medium, judged by its Hills, Bradys, Nadars, Atgets. So far did this tendency go that in 1889 P. H. Emerson wrote an obituary for photography as art, *The Death of Naturalistic Photography*. Believing the essense of art to be freedom from discipline and considering "the limitations of photography . . . so great," he consigned it to the circumscribed function of being "a true and literal scientific transcript of nature." In this judgment, Emerson himself expressed a mechanical attitude. To oppose his position, a new school of thought came into being, the pictorialist movement, led by Alfred Stieglitz.

No matter that today the word "pictorial" is held in disrepute by vanguard photographers. In its period, a half century ago, it represented a need and healthy reaction from Emerson's conception. To the pictorialists of 1890, photography was a medium of expression not inferior to painting or graphic art, but different. "Using the methods and materials which belong exclusively to photography, Stieglitz has demonstrated beyond doubt," wrote Paul Strand in *Mss.* in 1922, "that when the camera machine is guided by a very sensitive and deeply perceptive artist, it can produce perfectly embodied equivalents of unified thought and feeling. This unity may be called a vision of life—of forces taking form in life." In this view, the machine, the camera is "a new means of intellectual and spiritual enrichment." In the creative role of the human being using the camera, thus lay that freedom which Emerson felt was denied photography by its mechanical limitations.

In our period, revolt has again been necessary. Because the followers of the early pictorialists went so far astray from the legitimate bounds of photography, the only direction in which this revolt could take place was toward the technical and physical qualities of the medium, which might superficially be described as a return to Emerson's "literal scientific transscript of nature." In fact, we almost come back to the position implied in a press review of 1844, in which it is reported that "The plates of the present work are impressed by the agency of light alone, without any aid whatsoever from the artist's pencil." In discussing this rather complicated historical and philosophical subject, I do so to suggest the orientation of modern photography.

Photography is the medium par excellence of our time. As a visual means of communication, it has no equal. Because of its value and usefulness, we would be very bigoted and even irresponsible to seek to legislate a narrow perfectionism for the medium, though equally we have a duty to combat the false Ananias in photography as well as in art. If we can make an effective comment by cropping, dodging, spotting, distorting, that is certainly legitimate. Photomontage has great powers of communication, as may be observed in the work of John Heartfield. Impressionism in printing, that is, accentuating shadows, making them blacker by more contrasty manipulation or adjusting the general tone to a more psychological effect, may be accepted—though if the overemphasis on cloud effects in a single negative is to be deplored, what can be said of the unforgivable practice of faking in clouds by multiple printing! What to me is anathema—a corpse-like, outmoded hangover—is for photography to be a bad excuse for another medium. Anything that smacks of painting, charcoal drawing, etching, aquatint, is strictly forbidden. The slave mentality behind this falsification is the most dangerous and important objection. Is not photography good enough in itself, that it must be made to look like something else, supposedly superior? The first thing to leave behind as excess luggage is the notion that art is sacrosanct, that using oil paints makes the picture in itself art. What makes art is the man who feels, thinks, labors, sweats, dreams, hopes. This is as true with photography as any other medium.

All subject matter is open to interpretation, requires the imaginative and intelligent objectivity of the person behind the camera. The realization comes from selection, aiming, shooting, processing with the best technic possible to project your comment better. But devious manipulation into the falsified, "arty" "prettiness" of petty minds is certainly not a photographic function. Here Emerson was right: "Avoid prettiness," he wrote in 1886, "the word looks much like pettiness, and there is but little difference between them." He wrote too what may be adopted by photographers as a slogan and tacked up on the darkroom wall along with formulas: "The value of a picture is not proportionate to the trouble and expense it cost to obtain it, but to the poetry that it contains." The spontaneity of Cartier-Bresson's *Child at Play* creates this poetry of photography, as a thousand frozen miracles of technic could not. The expressive and esthetic impact of a photograph, one might add, is not the result of a cerebral determination to produce a work of art, but of a complex of factors, in which the suitability of the form to the function is certainly important. O'Sullivan's early photograph of *Cañon de Chelle, New Mexico,* 1873, proves the point. It is beautiful because it has fulfilled its use, recording the subject completely and understandingly.

In considering its application to present-day work, we can see that straight photography today exercises a corrective influence in two directions, against the kind of repetition of picturemaking extolled by the pictorialists who say flatly that they see no reason why a picture made in 1940 should be any different than one made in 1904, thereby ignoring the change in external environment, costume, transportation, let alone in human habits of thought and social association, and against the frivolousness of those who manipulate the medium purely for selfish ends, as in the surrealist nightmares before mentioned. Contrasted with the horrors of sentimentality and of pseudo-sophistication, straight photography is a clean breath of good, fresh air. It affirms again, as history and tradition do, the essential photogenic quality of photography and calls for the use of the medium without perversion of its true character.

Nevertheless, the limitations within which straight photography has been understood have in their turn generated revolt, the contemporary documentary movement which may be considered a revolt against the coldness and emptiness of human content of some straight photographs. There is a saturation point, as far as attention is concerned, in viewing still lifes of rocks, trees, sand, ferns and all the other subjects so minutely and exquisitely rendered by f/64's needle-sharp precision. We live in a world of human beings. Through daguerreotypes, calotypes, tintypes, family albums and all, photography has recognized this fact for a century. In news photography, lively and immediate application of the medium, the fact has never been forgotten. In "art" photography (so-called, though there should be an injunction against the phrase), humanity has too often been left out of the picture. The drive now is to get human beings back where they belong on the center of the stage.

66. ANCIENT RUINS IN THE CAÑON DE CHELLE, NEW MEXICO, 1873 T. H. O'SULLIVAN
Albumen print. Made by photographer on U. S. Geologic Survey, which may be called a document of nature, shows how photography has always been a "straight" medium.
Museum of Modern Art

67*a*. CHILD AT PLAY
HENRI CARTIER-BRESSON

Made with Leica. This spontaneous, poetic photograph is an expression of the spirit of straight photography, which is essentially honest and direct.

67*b*. ANGELS JOHN HEARTFIELD
Photomontage, created and controlled by the conscious artist, can be as much an expression of the ideals of straight photography as the needle-sharp, unmanipulated, unretouched prints of the f/64 school.

25. Documentary Photography

THE word "documentary" no less than "straight" has come to have a somewhat limited meaning when applied to photography. Yet its use in this connection is of such recent date that Webster's defines the adjective thus: "Consisting of, or in the nature, of documents; contained or certified in writing. Of or pertaining to, or employing, documentation in literature or art." Writing and art, yes, but no mention of photography, perhaps the most documentary of all mediums. The definition for the word "document" brings us closer to the meaning: "—in its most extended sense, including any writing, book, or other instrument conveying information."

In this sense, we may argue that all significant works of art in any medium are documents of their period, telling what kind of clothes people wore, how they sheltered themselves, even to a degree what their skeletal development was by their height measured against recognizable objects and by the shape of their faces. Certainly, works of art tell us not only about the manners and mores of their time, but also about the mind of their maker. In this respect, then, documents may be either objective or subjective, personal or social in character. In photography, the range of the document may be from photostats of disputed legal papers to such a highly personal and romantic expression as Stieglitz's cloud photographs, "conveying information" about cloud forms—cirrus, cumulus, nimbus or stratus—as well as about the photographer's inner emotional life.

We may have documents of nature, as in O'Sullivan's photograph of *Cañon de Chelle, New Mexico*, 1873 (Pl. 66), which has great value as a form of information about an important culture remain bound to change in the course of years, as well as great value for its esthetic quality and poetry. Porter's photographs of bird life and of nature are surely sources of information, as well as beautiful in themselves. There can be documents of people, like Nadar's portrait of Delacroix or Hill's calotypes of the life of fisherfolk in the village of Newhaven. Atget's photographs of Paris (see bibliography), made from before the beginning of the twentieth century till 1927, are documents of a civilization. As his friend, M. André Calmettes, wrote me, they record "*trésors et misères.*" They show the effect of man's hands and thought on his environment, as in the photograph of *Rockefeller Center*, 1932 (Pl. 49), under construction, the marks of compressed air drills on granite are as much a fact as the marks of wind and rain erosion in the New Mexican canyon. Without question, the documents of science made by photography of various kinds, stroboscope, high-speed X-ray, electronic microphotography, are notable not only for the facts they tell but also for a beauty which is a new esthetic expression.

What, then, is meant specifically by documentary photography in our time? There has been a tendency to confine the movement (which I have said was a necessary revolt from the lack of human content of much straight photography) to work of sociological purpose, to what James Thrall Soby in *U. S. Camera* magazine (No. 12) has described as "the desolation and horrors of poverty." Steichen, in writing about "The F.S.A. Photographers" in the 1939 *U. S. Camera* annual, emphasized the value of photographs expressing this subject matter with the brusque observation: "If you are the kind of rugged individualist who likes to say 'Am I my brother's keeper?,' don't look at these pictures—they may change your mind." The fine photographic pictures of Dorothea Lange and Paul S. Taylor, *An American Exodus*, has come out of this soil. Indeed from the beginning of the twentieth century, the United States has had a continuous history of photographers who sought to make the world better with their cameras, starting with that pioneer, Lewis W. Hine, as Elizabeth McCausland points out in her article, "Boswell of Ellis Island," in *U. S. Camera* magazine, No. 2.

However, there is some justice to Soby's plaint that all walks of life should be documented as well as the underprivileged third of a nation. *The Gambler* of Lisette Model (Pl. 42) is surely no less interesting as a revelation of human life than Russell Lee's *Old Woman's Hands* (Pl. 12), or Atget's "*Trésors et misères:*" *St. Cloud* (Pl. 70); than Max Yavno's New York slum, "*Desolation and Horrors of Poverty*" (Pl. 69). Beaumont Newhall's essay, "Documentary Approach to Photography," in the March, 1938, issue of *Parnassus*, states a broader conception and points out the many ways of usefulness as document in which photography may be put to work, at the same time stressing the organic esthetic quality needed to enhance the effectiveness of the documentary statement.

The battle of opinion which rages about documentary is paralleled in the discussion of the early days of pictorialism, chronicled in the pages of *Camera Notes* and *Camera Work,* as to whether or not photography is art. The prime quality of photography was well stated by Shaw in 1910, when he wrote:

"True, the camera will not build up a monumental fiction as Michael-Angelo did, or coil it cunningly into a decorative one, as Burne-Jones did. But it will draw it as it is, in the clearest purity or the softest mystery, as no draughtsman can or ever could. . . . Photography is so truthful—its subjects such obvious realities and not idle fancies—that dignity is imposed on it as effectively as it is on a church congregation."

The American painter George Luks, one of the early twentieth century group known as the "New York Realists," had this same sense of the realistic function of pictorial art when he asked how the future was to know what we looked like, what fire engines were like, or what kind of clothes we wore, unless the artist (for this, read "photographer") presented truthfully what he saw.

Taft, in *Photography and the American Scene,* describes the historical function of photography cogently:

"1. Such a photograph should truthfully record significant aspects of our material culture or environment, the development of such culture or environment, or any individual, incident, or scene of possible historic value. . . .

"2. The photograph should be properly documented. That is, the pictorial record should be accompanied by a suitable contemporary description or caption of the subject photographed, the name of the photographer should be given, and the date of recording should be given or established, so that collectively there is sufficient information to establish without question the authenticity of the photograph."

In my documentation of *Changing New York,* I sought to meet these criteria, the text by Elizabeth McCausland being planned to fulfil the second of Taft's requirements. The growing tendency to stress appendices of technical and related data in photographic books is part of the documentary movement, without doubt. This sort of information has the value for the future that the imprint of a book has, it locates the photograph in time and space.

The emphasis of documentary photography I have said lies, not on technical or external photographic performance in the spirit of art for art's sake, but on human content. This conception widens out into a further phase, stated by Lincoln Kirstein in *American Photographs* (see bibliography), as follows:

"The use of the visual arts to show us our own moral and economic situation has almost completely fallen into the hands of the photographer. . . . The facts of our homes and times, shown surgically, without the intrusion of the poet's or painter's comment or necessary distortion, are the unique contemporary field of the photographer, whether in static print or moving film. It is for him to fix and to show the whole aspect of our society, the sober portrait of its stratifications, their backgrounds and embattled contrasts. It is the camera that today reveals our disasters and our claims to divinity." Robert Disraeli, in his chapter "The Passing Scene," in *Miniature Camera Work,* amplifies the point.

It is significant that this function of photography was prophesied, as it were, by Balzac, writing in 1831 in *The Quest of the Absolute:*

"It so happens that human life in all its aspects, wide or narrow, is so intimately connected with architecture, that with a certain amount of observation we can usually reconstruct a bygone society from the remains of its public monuments. From relics of household stuff, we can imagine its owners 'in their habits as they lived.' Archeology, in fact, is to the body social somewhat as comparative anatomy is to animal organization. A complete order of things is implied by the skeleton of an ichthyosaurus. Beholding the cause, we guess the effect, even as we proceed from the effect to the cause, one deduction following another until a chain or evidence is complete, until the man of science raises up a whole bygone world from the dead, and discovers for us not only the features of the Past, but even the warts upon those features."

The reason I emphasize the content of documentary photography by these quotations is that I believe content to be the *raison d'être* of photography, as of all methods of communication. The importance of content is demonstrated by the fact that the photographs which have survived from the past and which ever increase in value and prestige are those endowed with content and documentary interest, as well as beauty. The primitive trestle bridge of Lincoln's time (see Brady's photograph, Pl. 18) is not a beautiful object, but it is certainly a beautiful photograph, because it tells us so poignantly about our country's technological birthpains: this is our past as Americans, organized in a most lucid manner.

The potentiality of the camera for communication of content is almost unlimited. The photograph, full of detail and objective, visual facts, speaks to all people. Where language barriers impede the flow of spoken or written ideas, the photograph is not handicapped; the eye knows no nation. Indeed, photography may be said to be another form of transportation, because it bridges oceans and continents, brings faraway lands close and shows us countries and peoples inaccessible to travel. With this important objective in mind, we ask "What is it that photography is to communicate? What content shall it state?" The answer is implicit in what has been stated before. Photography is to communicate the realities of life, the facts which are to be seen everywhere about us, the beauties, the absurdities, the achievements, the waste, of contemporary civilization.

Photography may speak of the wide miles of our American countryside, its waving wheatfields, its great mountains and canyons, surf on a thousand white beaches. It may speak, also, of slums, of those who are housed in inadequate and substandard dwellings without decent plumbing, heating or lighting. It may speak of American types—city-dwellers, sharecroppers, fruit pickers in Southern California, workers in factories, storekeepers, pushcart vendors, middle class clubwomen, national political conventions, an American Legion parade, cafe society, the Easter parade. Isolating the individual from the species, it may speak intimately and profoundly in the portrait, giving a revelation of character, a deep view into the ultimate mystery of human personality. Photography may speak of conflicting strata of society, our period superimposed on the previous, like one glacial age on the previous, setting down the culture morphology of a strange and bewildering world.

In other words, it is real life, the life you see everyday, which is exciting and worthy of note. When Brady made his thousands of negatives of the Civil War, he was photographing the *realest* thing that happened in his time, the acute struggle between two ways of life, the industrial and the agrarian. War, in all its horrors, was the outward and visible sign of conflict. In its wake, it left ravaged towns and fields, houses gutted by fire, dead bodies, abandoned trenches. Here is a profound and dreadful chapter in American history, set down in a profound and dreadful document.

Today, photographers have a world no less profound and dreadful to record. In this crisis of world history, it is important to understand clearly the potential function and value of the photographer as the historian of human life. To sum up, I may quote from Newhall's *Parnassus* article:

> "It is important to bear in mind that 'documentary' is an approach rather than an end. Slavish imitation of the style of other workers is meaningless. Photography has suffered from imitation almost more than the other arts; various movements have been so blindly followed that the force of the original impetus has been lost. 'Pictorialism' had a definite esthetic place so long as it was not practiced as an end; the Photo-Secessionists at the turn of the century were genuinely creative. Yet compare the plates of *Camera Work* with the prizewinners in pictorial salons today! The followers have imitated the form and the technic, but they have omitted the spirit of the original. Just within the last few years we have seen the growth of the 'candid' school from the truly amazing unposed portraits of Dr. Erich Salomon in the late 'twenties to the most casual snapshot by any one whose pocketbook can afford a miniature camera with an f/2 lens. Dr. Salomon's pictures were correctly described by the editor of a London illustrated paper as 'candid,' but the majority of similar photographs deserve no such adjective.
>
> "And so it is with 'documentary.' Because the majority of best work has been concerned with the homes and lives of the underprivileged, many pictures of the down-and-out have been made as 'documentaries.' The decay of man and of his buildings is picturesque; the texture of weathered boards and broken windowpanes has always been particularly delightful to photograph. Eighty years ago a critic in the *Cosmopolitan Art Journal* wrote: 'If asked to say what photography has best succeeded in rendering, we should point to everything near and rough.' These things, taken for their picturesqueness, may and often do form photographs of great beauty. But unless they are taken with a seriously sociological purpose, they are not documentary.
>
> "The documentary photographer is not a mere technician. Nor is he an artist for art's sake. His results are often brilliant technically and highly artistic, but primarily they are pictorial reports. First and foremost he is a visualizer. He puts into pictures what he knows about, and what he thinks of, the subject before his camera. Before going on an assignment, he carefully studies the situation which he is to visualize. He reads history and related subjects. He examines existing pictorial material for its negative and positive value—to determine what must be

re-visualized in terms of his approach to his assignment, and what has not been visualized.

"But he will not photograph dispassionately; he will not simply illustrate his library notes. He will put into his camera studies something of the emotion he feels toward the problem, for he realizes that this is the most effective way to teach the public he is addressing. After all, is not this the root meaning of the word 'document' (docere, 'to teach') ? For this reason, his pictures will have a different and more vital quality than those of a mere technician. They will even be better than those of a cameraman working under the direction of a sociologist, because he understands his medium thoroughly, and is able to take advantage of its potentialities while respecting its limitations."

From this point, we may proceed to a definition that the photography which best expresses the interplay of forces in our period will be a synthesis of straight and documentary, in which the excellent photogenic technic of the former school and the human emphasis of the latter will be fused. Before this can happen, there will need to be an improvement in materials and equipment; for much of the coldness and lack of action of straight photography has been due to the inability of existing film and lenses to capture human activity and at the same time give a reasonably good photograph. All these drives and objectives act as impetus to science and industry to produce better materials, which in turn should further encourage photographers.

26. Standards for Photography

IN discussing standards for photography, I do not wish to talk about the physical limitations of materials and equipment—the relatively slow speed of film, the clumsiness and flimsiness of cameras, the impermanence of papers—though these are legitimate subjects for inquiry. I wrote a lengthy "hymn of hate" on this subject some years ago in *Popular Photography* (May, 1939), and don't feel like repeating it. The recently formed committee on standards, which works from the point of view of research and production, should prove a good influence in raising the material standard of photography. What I am interested in is standards as they apply to the use and practice of photography. These are mental and emotional much more than physical. They are important, not abstractly in themselves, but because of their relation to the communicative purpose and content of photography.

As a starting point for a discussion of standards in photography, I may quote from Elizabeth McCausland's essay, "One Hundred Years of the American Standard of Photography," in the 1940 *U. S. Camera* annual:

"Mystical ecstacies aside, we may define photography in clean, neat terms, as it has been used during a hundred years on the American continent.

"What are the criteria garnered from this century?

"First: A good likeness; the daguerreotype. Truth to the subject, the sitter. Realism, honesty, the thing itself, not the photographer's subjective, introverted emotion about the thing.

"Second: Fidelity to materials, textures, as hair, gravel, silk. A prime beauty of photography, the minute rendering of textures.

"Third: A popular art. Dentists, tradesmen made daguerreotypes in their spare time. Millions of hobbyists today tote Brownies, Kodaks, Arguses.

"Fourth: Constant technical growth. Faster film, more sensitive meters, sturdier and lighter tripods, Polascopes. The effort of machinery to catch up with the imagination and the racing tempo of history.

"Fifth: Historical value. American Civil War. War—Spain; China; Europe. A baby crying in the streets. Sudden death from the skies. Missouri sharecroppers. Destitution on the rich American farmlands. Slums in the shadow of Wall Street. The future will be interested.

"Sixth: Quality. Better control of machine and material, not for quality's own sake, but to heighten communication.

"Seventh: Truthfulness. Honesty. Fidelity. "The camera cannot lie." But it can. Unless its user does not lie.

"Eighth: Technical standards. 'Straight' photography. 'Clear definition' and 'brilliancy and sharpness.'

"Ninth: Subject matter. Objective reality. The world today, the world in the grip of powerful forces, the world played upon by death, war, and famine. The world confronting crisis.

'Tenth: Multiple reproduction. The half-tone, the power press, the millions.

"Eleventh: For the future. An archive.

"Twelfth: Propaganda: for peace; for better housing; for public health; for civil liberties.

"Thirteenth: Science: for human betterment.

"Fourteenth: The dimension of time: action, motion. The tempo of our century, the acceleration of history."

The approach necessary to produce photographs which fulfil these standards is already well defined in the practice of fine workers. The Civil War photographs of Brady, the early twentieth century American documentary photographs of Lewis Hine, the Paris scenes of Atget, some of the photographs published in *Life*—these present, whether as the result of conscious intention on the photographer's part or as the result of sound intuition, the tradition of direct, realistic straight photography, where the camera is used simply and naturally as an instrument to record external reality. Here is the new esthetic of photography, based not on theories of trailing clouds, angle shots, gadgets, processes, but on what the camera can see and set down imperishably.

Technically, standards in photography derive from an exact yet imaginative knowledge of the camera. Learning the medium on a view camera or hand camera with ground glass is but the first step in a complex sequence. After the eye has been trained to see photogenically, after creative faculties have been disciplined to reject old conventions of the pictorial arts and to think and feel in terms of the photographic medium, then there is still much to do to achieve quality. One might be rash and say that the road to this goal would be made easier if we could have standardization and simplification, that much of what passes for photography today is needlessly complicated by a confusion of gadgets and of counsel, not to say sales talk.

Allied with the need for simpler and more standard methods is a psychological characteristic, which I believe is peculiar to Americans—a sort of overtechnical neurosis. I have already referred to this in the chapter on straight photography as an anti-technic revolution and instanced Cartier-Bresson as a photographer who in his work protested against too mechanical an approach to the medium. The American's respectful not to say subservient attitude toward technic is the direct opposite of that of the vanguard European photographers of a decade ago who threw over technic, cameras as machines, and shot willy-nilly their emotions onto light-sensitive gelatin emulsion, Cartier-Bresson, Germaine Krull, Eli Lotar, among them. Atget never trimmed a print in his life, to judge from the evidence of his almost 10,000 prints. If this is a spiritual antidote to a mechanical understanding and use of photography, more power to them, I say.

The division still seems to exist. Are Americans to put their feelings on a dusty shelf and tinker, tinker, eternally in the darkroom with that latest formula or film with which the clever manufacturer has so wilily seduced the shekels from our jeans? The slogan, "Technic for technic's sake," boils down to a cold, intellectualized, mechanized style. Actually, after technical mastery has been achieved, the photographer has only begun to approach his central problem. Technic for technic's sake is like art for art's sake—a phrase of artistic isolationism, a creative escapism. Technic in photography is like technic in industry, a means of doing something. In industry that something may be weaving cloth, mining coal, reaping wheat, generating electricity. In photography, the product is less tangible than a suit of clothes or a bag of flour or a ton of coal, but nevertheless equally useful and necessary to society.

In short, the something done by photography is *communication.* It was fashionable a dozen years ago to sneer at communication as the purpose of art and, indeed, even to deny that art has purpose. Non-intelligibility, non-communication were raised to ultimate ends. To say anything in a book, a picture, a piece of music, was anathema. The artist who did so was a prig and a prude and distinctly passé. That phase is past. With the rapid changes of history in recent years, serious artists do not haggle about what art is for or seek to abstain from human objectives in their work.

With this rebirth of interest in subject matter or content, which has had the effect of making realism the dominant mood today, vast numbers of people have been drawn—almost instinctively—to photography. Just as the most exciting reading matter is to be found in the daily newspapers, so in photographs we find the pictorial matter most sympathetic to the spirit of our age. This is because photography's direct, realistic nature is closely related to the scientific and technological forces which create the twentieth century's consummate speed and dynamics. From Nadar's minute-long poses to the split-second of candid portraiture is a measure of the present's accelerated tempo. Speed or telephone, telegraph, wireless, photoelectric eye, X-ray, TNT, airplane, stratosphere, round-the-world flights, have their visual counterpart in speed of lenses, shutters, film, the stroboscope, high-speed flash, electronic radiography.

The concrete image registered by the lens on film is comparable to the factual impact of contemporary reportage on the mind. We are conditioned to think and feel in headlines, in scraps of statistic, in slogans. Time moves, and life moves, with an irresistible rapidity. Who has time to be a Piranesi, faithfully setting down each crack in the stones of Rome in his engraved plates? Yet the romantic art of the nineteenth century will not satisfy the twentieth century. Emotion, rhetoric, Rembrandtesque light and shade, will not serve an age at the crossroads of history. Here the camera, inescapably realistic, fills our need. Prophets say that television will supplant the still photograph. That may be, though the radio has not yet supplanted the newspaper. But for the time being, photography answers the need of the present for a means of communication, straightforward, factual, documentary, scientific, realistic, truthful, honest.

What do these standards imply about a direction for photography in the future? I have written that photography is creating a new esthetic. This is based not only on perspective and plastic form as expressed by the lens, but also on the new subject matter made possible in our age by science. When the first stroboscopic photographs were exhibited, it was evident that in them was to be seen a *real* hyperreality, a true fantasy beyond what the subconscious could concoct. Some of Atget's photographs of reflections in Paris shop windows had had an intuitive premonition of the Bizarre juxtapositions of objects from nature which surrealism likes to flaunt, but with this difference—Atget's incongruities were seen and understood from life, not fabricated. They had the spontaneous absurdity or even madness of nature's chaos; they were not melancholy arrangements of the paranoiac vision. A step beyond this visual comment is the comment made by science when it sees the unseen, by means of all the most intricate and modern devices—the stroboscope and electronic radiography.

Here at last photography sees with its own eye, untouched by any memories of how painters saw in the past. For it is true, that in photographing subjects from life—people, buildings, landscape—we cannot help but be slightly influenced by the remembrance of how these subjects have been painted through the ages. The portraits of Hill and Mrs. Cameron are examples of how tradition imposed itself on the new art. The final liberation of photography from the past may come through the new subject matter of science, where there is no precedent for what is seen and photographed. No man before photography could know what an invisible particle of silver halide looked like. Enlarged 40,000 times, it is still less than two inches long. In these basic forms of materials may be found the new esthetic of photography.

I do not mean to suggest that photography will abandon its old subjects. By no means. Through centuries, pictures have used the same materials, because they are essential themes of human experience. I think of the new uses and the new themes—the unseen substances of life—as being a widening of the scope of photography, which will react to widen the imaginative approach of photographers to more usual subjects. For what our age needs is a broad, human art, as wide as the world of human knowledge and action; photography cannot explore too far or probe too deeply to meet this need.

68. THIS IS SUCH A FRIENDLY TOWN, 1913 LEWIS W. HINE

Contact print from 5 x 7 negative. Hine's intuitive sense of composition, discussed in Chapter 15, gives this social document added weight and meaning.

Courtesy of Corydon Hine

69. "DESOLATION AND HORRORS OF POVERTY" MAX YAVNO

Taken with 30-year-old 4 x 5 Century view; 6 inch Dagor lens; f/45; bulb opening and No. 2 Wabash flash bulbs and daylight; Super Panchro Press; Eastman D76; enlargement on Vitava Projection F2; developed in D72.

70. "TRÉSORS ET MISÈRES": ST. CLOUD — EUGÈNE ATGET

Document of a vanished world.

Collection of Berenice Abbott

71*a*. CUP OF COFFEE BREAKING

HAROLD E. EDGERTON AND K. J. GERMESHAUSEN

Stroboscopic photograph; about 1/100,000 seconds; f/16.

Courtesy of Massachusetts Institute of Technology

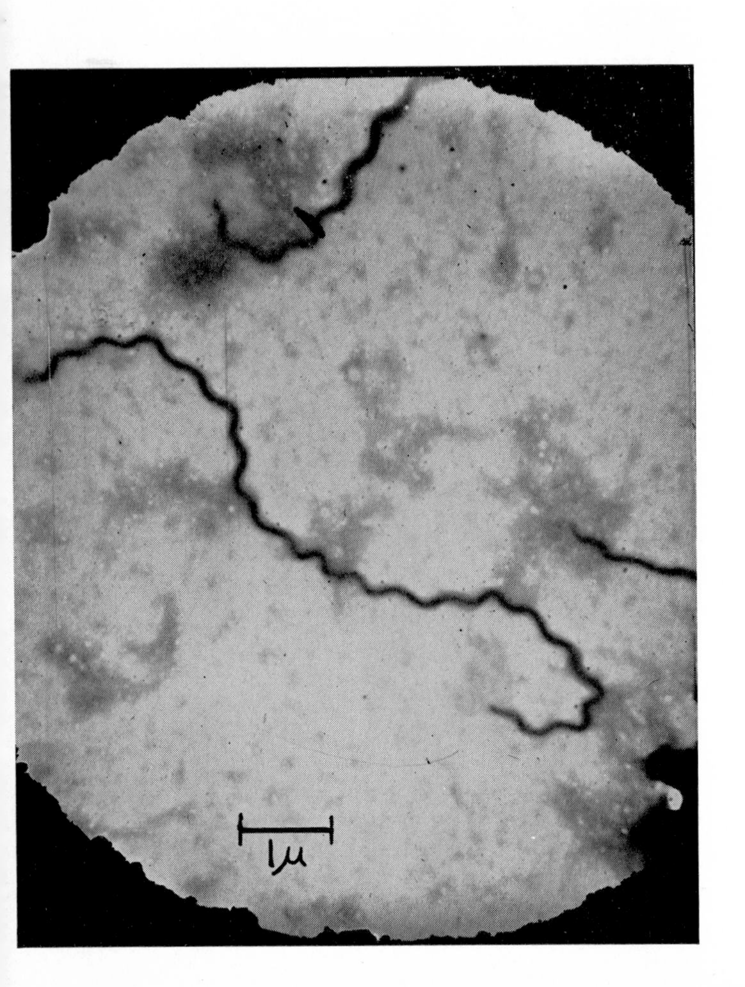

71*b*. LEPTOSPIRA CANICOLA

A spirochete which produces an infection in dogs. An electron micrograph, or electron picture, taken with an electron microscope produced by the RCA Manufacturing Company.

Courtesy of Dr. Harry E. Morton of the University of Pennsylvania and Dr. Thomas F. Anderson, RCA Fellow of the National Research Council

Bibliography

American Photographs. Walker Evans; with an essay by Lincoln Kirstein. New York: The Museum of Modern Art, 1938.

An American Exodus. Dorothea Lange and Paul S. Taylor. New York: Reynal & Hitchcock, 1939. "A record of human erosion."

Art of Retouching and Improving Negatives and Prints, The. (14th ed.) Robert Johnson; Arthur Hammond, rev. American Photographic Publishing Co. A last resort when the photographer has tried to produce a perfect negative without the use of any crutches and now wants to salvage something of his work.

Basic Photography. "Training Manual No. 2170-5," Air Corps, War Department. Write Superintendent of Documents, U. S. Government Printing Office, Washington, D. C., price 65 cents. The serious student can have no better reference work. A revised edition, to be issued as Technical Manual 1-221, is in preparation.

"Boswell of Ellis Island, The." Elizabeth McCausland in *U. S. Camera Magazine,* No. 2, 1939. A comprehensive account of the early work of Lewis W. Hine in photographing immigration at its heyday.

"Camera and the Eye, The." Alston Callahan, M.D., in *U. S. Camera Annual,* 1941, vol. 2, pp. 13 ff.

Changing New York. 97 photographs by Berenice Abbott; text by Elizabeth McCausland. New York: E. P. Dutton & Co., Inc., 1939.

Complete Photographer, The. General editor, Willard D. Morgan. New York: National Educational Alliance. Forthcoming publication to be announced. Will contain articles by the author of A GUIDE TO BETTER PHOTOGRAPHY and many of the photographers and writers on photography referred to in this book.

Dance Photographs of Martha Graham. Barbara Morgan. New York: Duell, Sloan & Pearce. [To be published late summer, 1941.] 150 photographs reproduced by gravure: a photographic repertory of 16 dances. Text: introduction by Barbara Morgan, essay on dance by Martha Graham, a biographical sketch by Frances Hawkins, and choreographic reference data by Louis Horst.

David Octavius Hill. H. Schwarz. New York: The Viking Press, 1931. Beautiful portraits by an early master, with documentary interest.

Death in the Making. Robert Capa. New York: Covici-Friede, 1938. A record of the War in Spain, in photographs, with running commentary.

"Eugène Atget." Berenice Abbott in *Creative Art,* Sept. 1929. The first article published in English on this French master, who photographed Paris for over thirty years till his death in 1927.

"Eugène Atget." Berenice Abbott in *U. S. Camera Magazine,* Nos. 12 and 13, 1940. A comprehensive biographical sketch.

Flash. Harold E. Edgerton and James R. Killian, Jr. Boston: Hale, Cushman and Flint, 1939. Photography with the help of the stroboscopic high speed flash technic.

"Flash Photography." Eliot Elisofon in *U. S. Camera Annual*, 1941, vol. I, pp. 177 ff. A practical article on multiple flash.

Graphic Graflex Photography. Willard D. Morgan, Henry M. Lester and twenty contributors. New York: Morgan & Lester, 1940. Contains chapter by Berenice Abbott on "The View Camera." Covers such subjects as elementary photography, exposure, lenses, filters, printing, Kodachrome, copying, dance, aerial, news, synchroflash, science, children, darkrooms, speedlamps, perspective, and identification photography.

"Iso Color Process." Paul Outerbridge. *U. S. Camera Magazine*, No. 15.

"Iso Color Process." Julius J. Wolfson. *Modern Lithography*, April 1941, Vol. 9, No. 4, pp. 34 ff.

Kodachrome and How to Use It. Ivan Dimitri. New York: Simon & Schuster, 1940. For color photography fans.

Leica Manual, The. Morgan & Lester and contributors. New York: Morgan & Lester, 1935. Covering all phases of miniature camera work, with especial emphasis on the Leica camera and its accessories. Subjects discussed include lenses, filters, films, enlarging, copying, projection, color, photomicrography, infrared, aerial, photomurals, news photography.

Men at Work. Lewis W. Hine. New York: The Macmillan Company, 1932. A pioneer documentary photographer's photographic chronicle of the construction of the Empire State Building.

Miniature Camera Work. Edited by Williard D. Morgan and Henry M. Lester. New York: Morgan & Lester, 1938. Out of print. To be issued in revised edition, with *Synchroflash Photography*, under new title, *Modern Camera Work*, in summer, 1941.

New Cameras and Photographic Equipment. Consumers Union Reports, August, 1939, pp. 21-28.

"100 Years of the American Standard of Photography." Elizabeth McCausland in *U. S. Camera Annual*, 1940, pp. 11-18. A panorama of a century by a leading art critic and writer on photography.

Photographic Buyers' Handbook, The. A. R. Lambert and Consumers Union. New York: Simon and Schuster, 1939. Compass and North Star to steer by in the wilderness of photographic gadgets.

Photographic Tanks: Tanks for Roll Film. Consumers Union Reports, August, 1940, pp. 9-11.

Photographing in Color. Paul Outerbridge. New York: Random House, 1940.

Photo-Lab-Index. Henry M. Lester. New York: Morgan & Lester, 1939. Basic set constantly brought up to date by quarterly supplements. "The Cumulative Formulary of Standard Recommended Photographic Processes." A two-volume looseleaf compilation, including processing formulas of all manufacturers, papers, filters, photographic lamps, conversion tables, film data, cine data, etc.

Photographs of Mexico. Paul Strand. New York: Virginia Stevens, 1940.

Photography and the American Scene. Robert Taft. New York: The Macmillan Company, 1938. Source materials for understanding the American tradition in photography.

Photography: A Short Critical History. Beaumont Newhall. New York: The Museum of Modern Art, 1938 (revised edition). A scholarly and provocative critique by a student of photography who has since become curator of the newly formed department of photography of the Museum of Modern Art.

Photography, Its Principles and Practice. C. B. Nebelette. New York: Van Nostrand, 1930. An excellent technical manual.

Photography: Theory and Practice. Louis Philippe Clerc. London: Pitman, 1930. A compendium of useful information.

Ratings of Exposure Meters: Photoelectric Exposure Meters. Consumers Union Reports, July 1940, pp. 7-9.

"Swing's the Thing." Edward J. Cook in *Photo Technique,* July and August, 1940. Well illustrated explanation of too often ignored adjustments on view and other ground glass cameras.

Synchroflash Photography. Willard D. Morgan. New York: Morgan & Lester, 1939. Out of print. To be issued in revised edition, with *Miniature Camera Work,* under new title, *Modern Camera Work,* in summer, 1941.

Wratten Light Filters. Eastman Kodak Co. 16th Ed., 1940.

You Have Seen Their Faces. Margaret Bourke-White and Erskine Caldwell. New York: Modern Age, 1937. Powerful documentary photographs and text, indicating the shameful poverty of the South.

Index